The Archaeology of the Hellenistic Far East: A Survey

Rachel Mairs

BAR International Series 2196
2011

Published in 2016 by
BAR Publishing, Oxford

BAR International Series 2196

The Archaeology of the Hellenistic Far East: A Survey

ISBN 978 1 4073 0752 7

© R Mairs and the Publisher 2011

The author's moral rights under the 1988 UK Copyright,
Designs and Patents Act are hereby expressly asserted.

All rights reserved. No part of this work may be copied, reproduced, stored,
sold, distributed, scanned, saved in any form of digital format or transmitted
in any form digitally, without the written permission of the Publisher.

BAR Publishing is the trading name of British Archaeological Reports (Oxford) Ltd.
British Archaeological Reports was first incorporated in 1974 to publish the BAR
Series, International and British. In 1992 Hadrian Books Ltd became part of the BAR
group. This volume was originally published by Archaeopress in conjunction with
British Archaeological Reports (Oxford) Ltd / Hadrian Books Ltd, the Series principal
publisher, in 2011. This present volume is published by BAR Publishing, 2016.

Printed in England

BAR titles are available from:

	BAR Publishing
	122 Banbury Rd, Oxford, OX2 7BP, UK
EMAIL	info@barpublishing.com
PHONE	+44 (0)1865 310431
FAX	+44 (0)1865 316916
	www.barpublishing.com

CONTENTS

CONTENTS	1
PREFACE	3
FIGURES	4
Figure 1: The Hellenistic East	5
Figure 2: Hellenistic Bactria-Sogdiana	6
Figure 3: Ai Khanoum	7
CHAPTER 1: THE HELLENISTIC FAR EAST	8
1.1 Scope	8
1.2 Chronological and Geographical Parameters	9
1.3 Resources, Limitations and Future Publications	10
CHAPTER 2: THE HISTORICAL TRADITION	12
2.1 Modern Histories of the Hellenistic Far East	12
2.2 Greek and Latin Sources	12
2.3 Indian and Chinese Sources	12
2.4 A Medieval European Tradition?	12
2.5 Early Modern Historical Studies	12
2.6 Historical Fiction	13
2.7 Cinema	13
CHAPTER 3: CULTURE AND IDENTITY IN THE HELLENISTIC FAR EAST	14
3.1 The Hellenistic Far East: Cultural Custody Battles	14
3.2 Theory and Archaeological Practice	15
3.2.1 The Colonial Hellenistic Far East	15
3.2.2 Ethnicity	15
3.2.3 Movement of Objects and Transformations in Meaning	16
3.2.4 Space and Landscape	17
3.2.5 Places in Between: The Postcolonial Hellenistic Far East	17
3.2.6 Multilingualism and Administration	18
CHAPTER 4: GENERAL PUBLICATIONS	20
4.1 Introduction	20
4.2 Synthetic Historical Studies	20
4.3 Edited Volumes	21
4.4 Exhibition Catalogues	21
4.4.1 The National Museum, Kabul	21
4.4.2 Loans from the National Museum, Kabul	21
4.4.3 Other Exhibitions of Central Asian Material	22
4.5 Numismatics	22
CHAPTER 5: ARCHAEOLOGY	23
5.1 Introduction	23
5.1.1 History of Archaeological Research	23
5.1.2 Problems and Methodologies	23
5.1.3 Research Tools and Thematic Studies	23
5.2 Sites: Bactria, Sogdiana, Margiana, Chorasmia	24

      5.2.1 Takht-i Sangin and the North-East ... 24
      5.2.2 Ai Khanoum and its Hinterland ... 26
      5.2.3 Bactra and its Oasis ... 29
      5.2.4 Termez, the Surkhan-darya and the North-West ... 30
      5.2.5 Derbent – The 'Iron Gates' ... 32
      5.2.6 Maracanda – Samarkand – Afrasiab ... 33
      5.2.7 Alexandria Eschate – Khujand ... 33
      5.2.8 Herat and Areia ... 34
      5.2.9 Merv and Margiana ... 34
      5.2.10 Chorasmia ... 34
   5.3 South of the Hindu Kush: The Kabul Region, Arachosia and India ... 34
      5.3.1 Begram ... 34
      5.3.2 Old Kandahar – Alexandria in Arachosia ... 35
      5.3.3 Gandhāra and Northwestern India ... 35
      5.3.4 India ... 37

CHAPTER 6: LANGUAGES AND TEXTS ... 38
   6.1 Overview ... 38
   6.2 Greek ... 38
      6.2.1 Corpora, Bibliographies and General Works ... 38
      6.2.2 Stone Inscriptions ... 38
      6.2.3 Texts on Durable Materials (Ceramics, Bricks, etc.) and Graffiti ... 39
      6.2.4 Texts on Papyrus and Skin ... 40
   6.3 Aramaic ... 41
      6.3.1 Stone Inscriptions ... 41
      6.3.2 Texts on Durable Materials (Ceramics, Bricks, Seals, etc.) and Graffiti 42
      6.3.3 Texts on Papyrus and Skin ... 42
   6.4 Other Languages (Prākit, Bactrian, Unidentified) ... 42
      6.4.1 Unidentified ... 42
      6.4.2 Prākit / Middle Indo-Aryan ... 42
      6.4.3 From Greek to Bactrian ... 42

CHAPTER 7: ONLINE RESOURCES ... 44
   7.1 Updates to the Hellenistic Far East Bibliography ... 44
   7.2 Portals and Collections of Material ... 44
   7.3 Publications ... 44
   7.3 Field Projects ... 44
      7.3.1 Afghanistan ... 44
      7.3.2 Uzbekistan ... 44
      7.3.4 Turkmenistan ... 45
      7.3.5 Pakistan ... 45
   7.4 Field Archaeologists' Webpages ... 45
   7.5 Museum Collections and Exhibitions ... 45
   7.6 Other Relevant Sites ... 45
   7.7 Texts ... 46

BIBLIOGRAPHY ... 47

PREFACE

This book has its origins in a PhD thesis completed at the University of Cambridge (*Ethnic Identity in the Hellenistic Far East*, Mairs 2006a), or rather in the formidable information-gathering exercise which had to be undertaken before that thesis could be written. My thesis was written under the supervision of Dr. Dorothy J. Thompson, to whom I am extremely grateful for her guidance and support, and examined by Professors Robin Osborne and Simon Hornblower.

My thanks also go to Professor Roger Bagnall of the Institute for the Study of the Ancient World, New York University, and the Warden, Professor Dame Jessica Rawson, and Fellows of Merton College, Oxford, for giving me the luxury of more years of full-time research than I could reasonably have hoped for. Among others, I have benefited greatly from discussions with Drs. Alice Stevenson (Oxford), Jennifer Gates-Foster (Texas) and Matthew Canepa (Minnesota), and on Chinese matters, Dr. Rod Campbell (Oxford). Dr. Omar Coloru (Paris) very kindly sent me a PDF of his 2009 monograph on the Greek kingdom of Bactria, when it was not yet available in the library at Oxford. The Directors and staff of the Turkmen-Italian Archaeological Map of the Murghab Delta project (I owe especial thanks to Lynne Rouse) and of the Minaret of Jam Archaeological Project made it possible for me to do fieldwork in Central Asia.

Love and thanks go, as ever, to my parents, grandparents and sisters.

FIGURES

1. The Hellenistic East. (Adapted from F. L. Holt 1999.)

2. Hellenistic Bactria-Sogdiana. (Adapted from F. L. Holt 1999.)

3. Ai Khanoum.

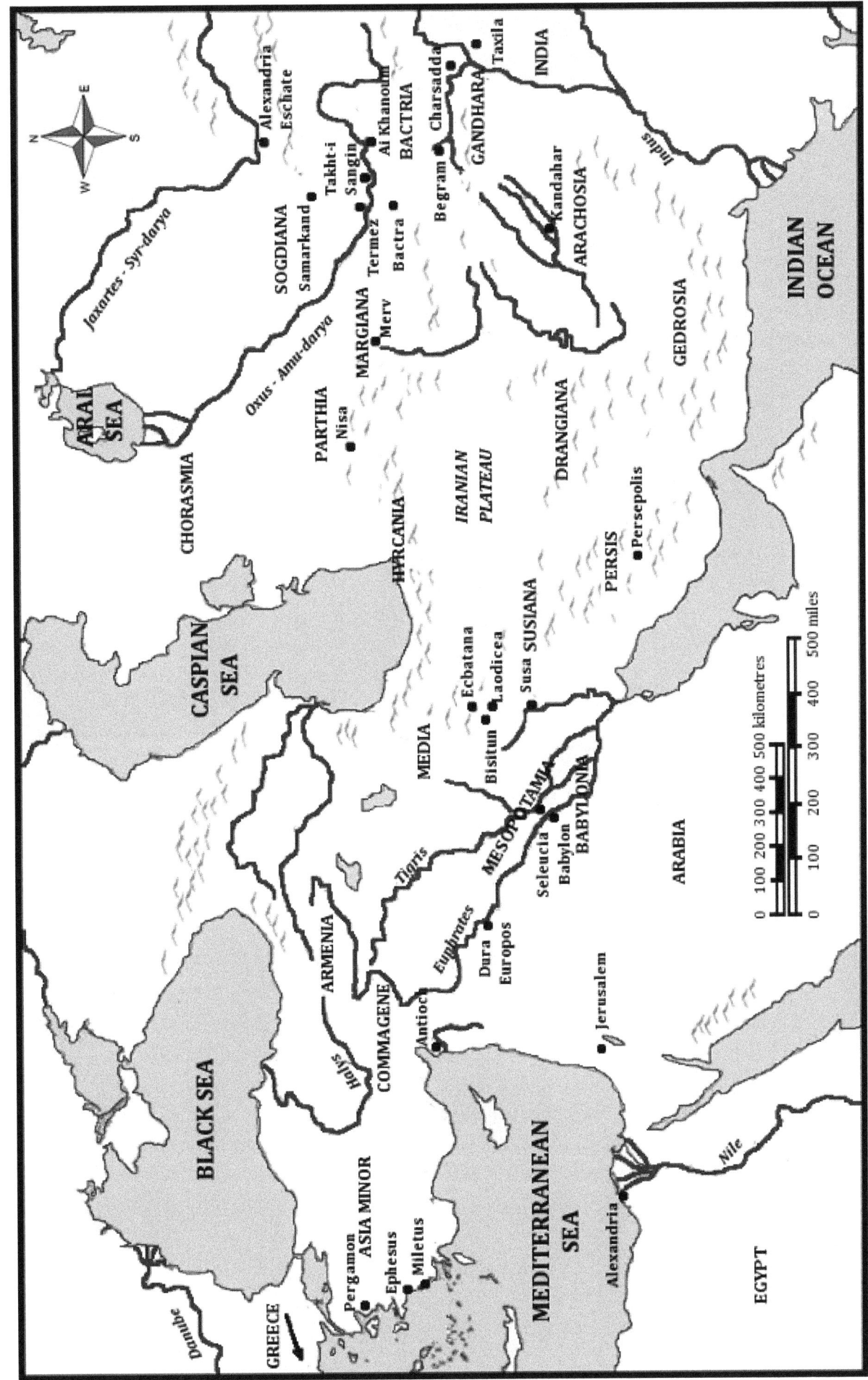

Figure 1: The Hellenistic East (Adapted from F. L. Holt 1999.)

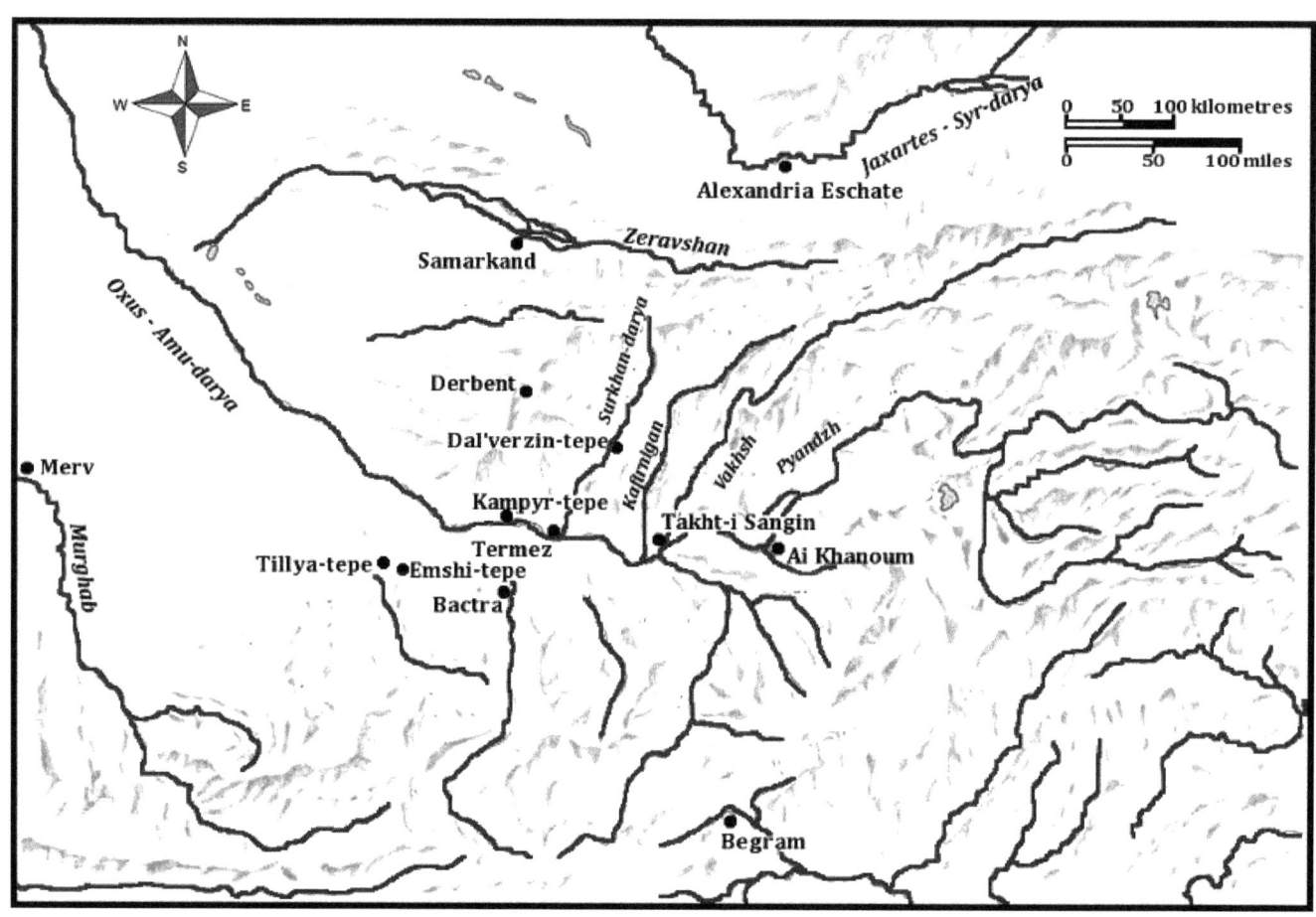

Figure 2: Hellenistic Bactria-Sogdiana
(Adapted from F. L. Holt 1999.)

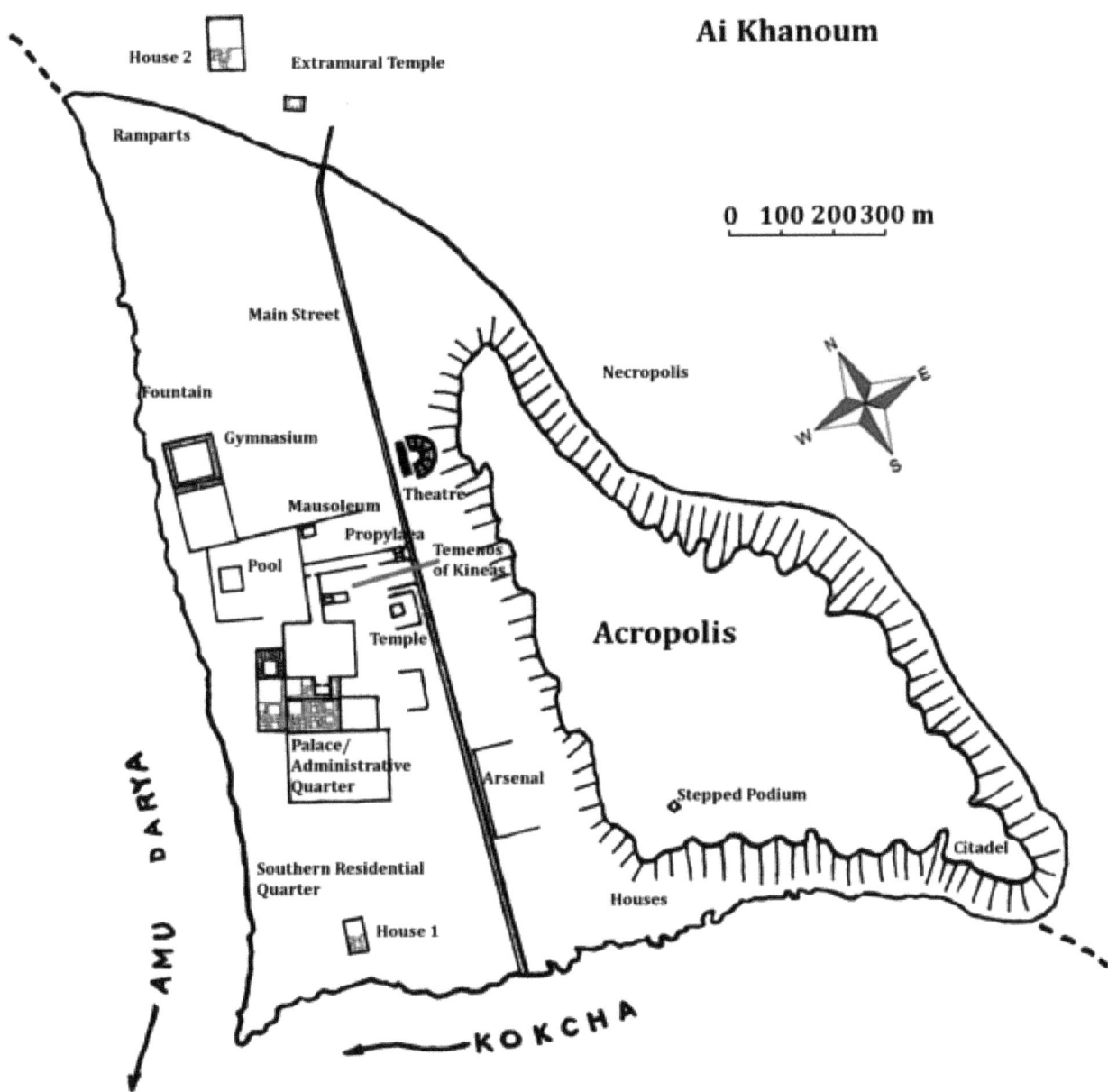

Figure 3: Ai Khanoum

CHAPTER 1
THE HELLENISTIC FAR EAST

1.1 Scope

This book is intended as an introduction to the archaeology of the easternmost regions of Greek settlement in the Hellenistic period, from the conquests of Alexander the Great in the late fourth century BC, through to the last Greek-named kings of north-western India somewhere around the late first century BC, or even early first century AD. The geographical and chronological parameters of this handbook are not stringently defined. The deficiencies of our evidence, and geo-political realities, make any attempt at such precision unwise and, indeed, potentially misleading.

The 'Far East' of the Hellenistic world – a region comprising areas of what is now Afghanistan, Pakistan, Iran and the former-Soviet Central Asian Republics – is best known from the archaeological remains of sites such as Ai Khanoum, which attest the endurance of Greek cultural and political presence in the region in the three centuries following the conquests of Alexander the Great. The 'Hellenistic Far East' (HFE) has become the standard catch-all term for a network of autonomous and semi-autonomous Greek-ruled states in the region east of the Iranian Plateau, which remained in only intermittent political contact with the rest of the Hellenistic world to the west – although cultural and commercial contacts could at times be very direct. These states, their rulers and populations, feature only occasionally in Greek and Latin historical sources. The two great challenges of HFE studies lie in integrating scholarship on this region into work on the Hellenistic world as a whole in a more than superficial way; and in understanding the complex cultural and ethnic relationships between the dominant Greek elites of the region and their neighbours, both within the Greek kingdom of Bactria and in its Central Asian hinterland.

A third problem in studies of the Hellenistic Far East – and one which is intimately connected to the two methodological issues already outlined – is the lack of a 'go-to' reference work which might make the region and its archaeology accessible both to archaeologists and historians who work on other regions of the Hellenistic world, and to those, especially more junior scholars, seeking to develop a research profile in the area. The latter problem is particularly acute: at present, many graduate theses are forced to replicate the same introductory, summary work, and cannot therefore devote as much time and space to more detailed archaeological case studies as might be hoped. There currently exists no up-to-date general reference work on the archaeology of this region. Earlier studies tended to be more historical or numismatic in focus, and are in any case now seriously outdated (Tarn 1951, 1st edition 1938; Narain 1957). The best recent studies still tend to take an approach which is fundamentally historical or numismatic, and it is intended that the present work will provide a complement to these (see further Chapter 4, Section 4.2). In addition, there are very few publications on the archaeology of the HFE in English: French predominates for Afghanistan and Iran, and – a far greater barrier to accessibility for European and North American readerships – almost all the primary archaeological publications on the states of former-Soviet Central Asia are in Russian and have not been translated into western European languages. (There are some notable exceptions among synthetic studies, such as Staviskij 1986 on Kushan Bactria, a French translation and revision of Staviskii 1977.) Although this language barrier will continue to prevent those without a knowledge of Russian from undertaking extensive research into the Hellenistic states of Central Asia, it is hoped that the present work will provide sufficient basic information and bibliographical references on current archaeological activities in the region for European and American scholars to make productive use of and reference to developments in Central Asian archaeology. Russian works are cited in the Bibliography along with an English translation of the title.

The model for this project – although the present work is on a much more modest scale – is the *Bulletin d'Histoire Achéménide* (*BHAch*), a structured reference guide to the history and archaeology of the Achaemenid Empire, which summarises current research and provides a comprehensive bibliography of recent works relevant to Achaemenid studies ('Outils de la recherche' > 'Bibliographies' at <http://www.achemenet.com/>, accessed 16 November 2010; its genesis is discussed in Briant 2002, xv-xviii). As well as providing a comprehensive and user-friendly resource on the current state of historical and archaeological scholarship on the Achaemenid Empire, a great virtue of the *BHAch* is its structure. The information presented is clearly organised into numbered sections and sub-sections, arranging material thematically according to the basic structure of Pierre Briant's *Histoire de l'Empire Perse* (Briant 1996; English translation: Briant 2002). Subsequent updates contain material ordered into sections numbered in the same way.

The present work consists of a series of short introductory essays on various aspects of the archaeology and history of the Hellenistic Far East, structured thematically and by category of evidence, with a gazetteer of archaeological sites by region, and inscriptions and documentary texts by language and medium. This initial volume will summarise, with critical commentary, archaeological work on the HFE to date. Current archaeological field projects will also be discussed. Like the *BHAch*, it is my intention to publish regular updates to the initial volume, in print and online. These updates which will follow the same, numbered format, with the intention that they may therefore be readily integrated with it.

A final word of caution: this introductory 'user's guide' claims to be nothing more than what it is. Its purpose is not primarily to provide a new summary or re-evaluation of cultural interactions in Greek Central Asia. It aims to answer a more basic, practical need. One of the greatest challenges facing scholars and students of the Hellenistic Far East is a rather prosaic one: the difficulty of collating their data. For those coming from a Classical background, as most still do, assembling a fairly comprehensive bibliography of archaeological publications and wider studies on Ai Khanoum is not difficult. Smaller sites, however, can often fly beneath the radar even of the most scrupulous, since they may have yielded limited (but still useful) material, and because they may be referenced only occasionally in the better known and more accessible publications. The small number of scholars who maintain an active research profile in the field – still fewer outside France or Central Asia – means that, at present, many theses and dissertations on the region are written by students who are working in intermittent contact with specialists. This means that the study of the Hellenistic Far East, such as it is, has resisted becoming ghettoised, and that students bring to the subject a wider historical or archaeological training, but it also means that they replicate much of the same basic introductory work. It is intended that the reader will use this book as a starting-point for research into a particular archaeological site or theme and follow up the references given. I have deliberately not, for example, included a detailed study of the city of Ai Khanoum and my discussion should not be cited as such. The goal of this handbook is to make the archaeology of this region accessible and 'usable', and at present the most useful step which can be taken towards this is, I believe, the collation of information and bibliographical data on our basic sources of evidence.

1.2 Chronological and Geographical Parameters

Much of the appeal of the term 'Hellenistic Far East' is that it is non-specific. Several regions of Central and South Asia came under Greek rule or influence in the Hellenistic period, but the nature and duration of this Greek presence varied. Bactria-Sogdiana, for example, became the centre of an independent Greek-ruled kingdom under the Diodotids in the mid-third century BC; Arachosia passed under Indian political control in the very late fourth century BC, yet continued to produce Greek inscriptions during the third century, before passing under Graeco-Bactrian control in the second, when the Greek rulers of Bactria instigated a process of military expansion into North-West India. Numismatic evidence attests Greek-named kings in the Panjab as late as the first century AD. The cultural and political connections between these regions makes some catch-all term useful, particularly if they are to be dealt with from a wider Hellenistic perspective. 'Hellenistic Far East' – or variants such as 'Greek Far East' and 'Hellenistic Farther East' – is

not a perfect solution, but its recurrence in the scholarly literature of several languages, and the lack of prejudice (so far) attached to its use, make it a convenient compromise. The term was apparently coined by Hassoulier in 1902, as 'Extrême-Orient grec' (on which see Schmitt 1990, 42, and Schlumberger 1960). Canali de Rossi's (2004) compendium of Greek inscriptions from the 'Estremo Oriente Greco' has brought the term into wider scholarly circulation. I prefer the term 'Hellenistic' – which I understand in both a political sense, referring to territory ruled by kings of ultimate Greek origin, and in a cultural sense as implying contact and interaction between Greek and non-Greek – to 'Greek', because while the cultural 'Greekness' of the region is a matter of some debate, the political and ideological inheritance of the kings of Bactria, and their later successors in Arachosia and India, is solidly Hellenistic, and their culture a typically Hellenistic mongrel, mixture, fusion, creole or hybrid (see Chapter 3).

I will make occasional reference to archaeological and textual material from the period of Achaemenid rule, in particular where this may be used to demonstrate long-term cultural and socio-economic continuities (to be discussed further in Mairs forthcoming-a), but my focus is on the period after Alexander. On Achaemenid Central Asia, see in particular Briant 1984; Briant 1985; Lyonnet 1990; and Francfort 2005. Canali De Rossi 2007 gives an account of the evidence for Greeks in Central Asia, and the Near East in general, under the Persian Empire, and Widemann 2001 starts his run-through of the political history of the Hellenistic Far East with the evidence for Greek settlement under the Achaemenids. The new Aramaic documents from Bactria, subject of a preliminary publication in Shaked 2004 and discussed in Chapter 3, Section 3.2.6, and Chapter 6, Section 6.3.3.1, below, will add greatly to our understanding of the Achaemenid imperial presence in Central Asia.

Alexander's conquests in the Upper Satrapies of the Persian Empire, which began in 330 BC, provide the 'start date' for this study. On Alexander's campaigns and routes in the East, see, inter alia: Stein 1929; Oikonomides 1980; Paul Bernard 1982a; Holt 1988, discussed by Bernard 1990; Dani and Bernard 1994; Bosworth 1996; Grenet and Rapin 1998a; Leriche 2002; Shihab 2002; Leeming 2003; Holt 2003; Holt 2005; Rapin 2005; Bopearachchi and Flandrin 2005; Reiss-Engelhorn-Museen 2009.

At the other end of the chronological scale, it is more difficult to find a convenient cut-off point. As in the Mediterranean world, the Hellenistic period in the Hellenistic Far East 'ended' at different times, and, as already outlined above, regions such as Arachosia might pass in and out of nominal 'Greek' political control. North of the Hindu Kush, nomadic incursions in the mid-second century BC, attested archaeologically at sites such as Ai Khanoum, put an end to the Graeco-Bactrian state. South of the Hindu Kush, and in particular in north-western India, Indo-Greek kings ruled until over a century later. From the first century AD, the Kushan Empire brought political unity to the region. The material culture, religious iconography and even written script of the Kushans owe much to the states of the Hellenistic Far East. It is therefore desirable to provide some coverage of things Kushan, but those looking for an account of any depth – or, indeed, adequacy – should look elsewhere (in particular, to the Kushan sections of Harmatta, et al. 1994 and to Staviskij 1986, an expanded French translation of Staviskii 1977).

It has become customary to refer to the Greek kingdoms north of the Hindu Kush as 'Graeco-Bactrian' and those in the Indian Subcontinent as 'Indo-Greek'. These designations are, for obvious reasons, unsatisfactory. The same dynasties or the same individual kings are often involved: at what point does the Graeco-Bactrian king Demetrios I, conqueror of India but attested in an inscription from northern Bactria (Chapter 6, Section 6.2.2.1: Kuliab), become 'Indo-Greek'? The conventional distinction between the two terms is intended to be (loosely) chronological and geographical, and the flexibilty in their usage should be borne in mind.

Geographical vagueness is also somewhat inevitable. The archaeological geography of the region will be discussed in more detail in Chapter 5, Section 5.2. In both ancient and modern usage, names such as 'Bactria' or 'Sogdiana' do not generally correspond to clearly demarcated entities on the ground. It is notable that the Classical sources preferred to refer to peoples rather than to territorial units ('Satrap of the Arachotians' rather than 'satrap of Arachosia': Arrian 3.28.1; cf. Staviskij 1986, 47, on Bactria and Bactrians). As used by Soviet archaeologists, 'Bactria' was extended from its usual ancient definition as the region south of the Oxus, to include areas farther north, thus emphasising the high degree of cultural uniformity found in archaeological material from the region. This modern definition of 'Bactria' makes a great deal of sense in archaeological terms and has come into widespread use. It is also apparent that the inconsistent attempts of the Classical sources to delineate a boundary between Bactria and Sogdiana along the Oxus did not reflect contemporary local conditions (Staviskij 1986, 47-55; Leriche 1985, 67; see further the discussion of the 'Iron Gates' at Derbent, Chapter 5, Section 5.2.5).

I will not discuss finer points of chronology, nor the ancient names of cities such as Ai Khanoum and Termez for which we have no real local epigraphic or other archaeological evidence (on the ancient name of Ai Khanoum, see the arguments presented in Bernard and Francfort 1978, 3-15, Narain 1986, Leriche 2007, 121-124, and Claude Rapin 2003; on Termez, Leriche 2002). If I make only occasional reference to the proposed dates of archaeological sites and inscriptions, and to matters of chronology in general, it is because so much is uncertain. The reader is referred to the debates contained in the bibliography cited.

1.3 Resources, Limitations and Future Publications

In addition to the traditional print resources, web resources now provide many convenient points of access both to old material and to up-to-date information on research and current archeological activities. I make reference to many of these in the text itself and provide a more comprehensive listing, including some additional resources, in Chapter 7. Even Wikipedia (<www.wikipedia org>), it must be confessed, appears to have attracted a fairly high quality of articles on the history, numismatics and archaeology of the Hellenistic Far East, although naturally as a source it must be treated with extreme caution.

The problem of actually locating the publications to which I refer in the following chapters in libraries or in bookshops remains, but electronic publication has made this task rather less frustrating than it was even five years ago. The excellent, free *Persée* portal (<www.persee.fr>), for example, offers access to all the Ai Khanoum reports originally published in the *Comptes-rendus de l'Académie des inscriptions et belles-lettres*, as well as in other journals such as the *Bulletin de Correspondance Hellénique* and *Bulletin de l'École Française d'Extrême Orient*. Google Books (<http://books.google.com>) and JSTOR (<www.jstor.org>, by subscription) offer access, in particular, to some of the less-numerous English-language materials on the region. Some projects, such as the *International Pluridisciplinary Archaeological Expedition to Bactria* (Chapter 5, Section 5.2.4: The Surkhan-darya Valley – Survey and GIS), now publish their reports online. Other archaeological missions in the region, such as the *Délégation Archéologique Française en Afghanistan* (DAFA: <www.dafa.org.af>) or the *Karakalpak-Australian Expedition* (<http://sydney.edu.au/arts/uscap/uzbekistan/index.shtml>), maintain web pages with less compendious, but still very useful, data.

A few words must be said about languages. The vast majority of publications on the region, both primary archaeological reports and subsequent studies, are in French or Russian. Some works, but not as many, are in English. A very small number of publications are in German or Italian. The divide between French and Russian scholarly publications lies roughly along the Oxus and the border between Afghanistan and the former-Soviet Central Asian Republics. A few collections of articles by Soviet and French scholars are available in French (Chapter 4, Section 4.3), and there has been much recent French-Uzbek collaboration. So a researcher with French but little or no Russian may reasonably expect to be able to work on material from Afghanistan and the Indo-Iranian borderlands, but for anyone who wishes to work on the regions north of the Oxus a reading knowledge of Russian is still essential. Some Russian articles carry a summary in French or English (for example, those in the journal *Vestnik Drevnei Istorii*), but most do not.

I have tried to make the bibliography as comprehensive as possible with the library and other resources available to me. I hope that my debt to other sources of information, especially the bibliographical data available on the personal webpages of many scholars (see listing in Chapter 7), will be clear. As well as very new publications, many older ones, especially those published in the post-Soviet states of Central Asia or in out-of-the-way journals, have certainly escaped my notice. In particular, the series *Афрасяб* (*Afrasiab*) and *История материальной культуры Узбекистана* (*Istoriya material'noii kul'tury Uzbekistana*: *IMKU*) were not available to me (there is an online table of contents for *IMKU* at <http://kronk.narod.ru/library/imku.htm>, accessed 16 October 2010). For this reason, it is likely that my information on some sites, especially the smaller ones, is out-of-date or inaccurate. References should therefore always be followed up where possible in the original publications. I have been as careful as I can in noting where I have not personally been able to inspect the publications in question.

A step towards remedying this situation will, I hope, be made in the compilation of regular updates of new material, or material which has escaped my intention, to be published, primarily online, following the same chapter and section numbering schema as used in this book. These updates will be made available on the website <www.bactria.org> and, for users of Academia.edu, at <http://oxford.academia.edu/RachelMairs>.

CHAPTER 2
THE HISTORICAL TRADITION

2.1 Modern Histories of the Hellenistic Far East

This chapter presents only a very brief skeleton-summary of the ancient and modern historical and literary traditions on the Hellenistic Far East. For a full account, Coloru 2009 should be consulted: given the fullness of the references in this new synthesis, I have not attempted anything approaching comprehensiveness here (on Coloru 2009, complemented by Widemann 2009, see Chapter 4, Section 4.2).

For recent historical and synthetic studies of the Hellenistic Far East, see also Chapter 4, Section 4.2.

2.2 Greek and Latin Sources

The Greek and Latin historical sources on the Hellenistic Far East are collected in Appendix D to F. L. Holt 1999, and discussed in the works already cited above. They are few and far between. No account of any length survives, although such accounts, such as in the *Historiae Philippicae* of Pompeius Trogus epitomised by Justin, did once exist. Polybios' treatment (10.49; 11.34) of the siege of Bactra by Antiochos III offers the most informative narrative. Karttunen 1999/2000 summarises the Greek and Latin sources on one particular figure, the Graeco-Bactrian king Eucratides.

2.3 Indian and Chinese Sources

Karttunen 1997, and for earlier periods Karttunen 1989, collects and discusses the sources on Greek dealings with India – and Indian dealings with the Hellenistic world – both before and after the conquests of Alexander (Hellenistic diplomacy with India: Karttunen 1997, 69-94). On the Greek Edicts of Aśoka at Kandahar, and the epigraphic presence of Greeks in northern and central India, see Chapter 6, Sections 6.2.2.2, 6.3.2.2 and 6.4.2.

The Indo-Greek king Menander makes a famous appearance in a Pāli Buddhist text of around 100 BC, the *Milindapañha* (trans. Rhys-Davids 1890 and Horner 1963-4). This purports to be a dialogue between King 'Milinda' and a Buddhist sage named Nāgasena, and concludes with the king's conversion to Buddhism (the historicity or otherwise of this episode is discussed by Bopearachchi 1990a).

Given the extension, over time, of the terms *Yona* (Prākrit) or *Yavana* (Sanskrit) to mean any generic 'westerner', it is often difficult to differentiate inhabitants of the Graeco-Bactrian and Indo-Greek kingdoms in Indian sources from their later north-western successors, or even seafaring visitors from the Roman Empire. Karttunen 1994 discusses Yonas and Yavanas in inscriptions, and Ray 1988 evaluates their presence in ancient India. On foreigners (*mlecchas*), including Greeks, and their reception in Indian society, see Parasher 1991, who provides a nuanced and sociologically-informed treatment of the relevant Indian literary texts. Older works, now of primarily historiographical interest, include Banerjee 1919 and Jairazbhoy 1963.

The Chinese sources on contact with the Greek world are evaluated in Kordosis 1994. This work should be read with caution, as per the critical review of F. G. Naerebout in *Mnemosyne* 49.3 (1996), 373-377, which questions Kordosis' command of the Chinese sources. The major Chinese travellers' accounts of Bactria post-date the fall of the Graeco-Bactrian kingdom in the mid-second century BC (see e.g. the reports of the imperial envoy Zhang Qian, as recorded in the *Shiji*, compiled by Sima Qian in the first century BC: trans. Watson 1993; the relevant portion is *Shiji* 123, pages 231-252 of the translation). For further discussion of Bactria at this period, including the Chinese sources, see Posch 1995.

2.4 A Medieval European Tradition?

The appearance of "grete Emetreus, the kyng of Inde", i.e. the Graeco-Bactrian invader of India, Demetrios I, in Chaucer's *Knight's Tale* (I 2155-2159) is a curiosity, but it has proven difficult to trace Chaucer's sources of information. It is possible that he drew on some lost medieval tradition (Bivar 1950, for example, traces this through Boccaccio). It seems to me equally likely that, should any Graeco-Bactrian coins have been known in Europe at this time, any learned or popular impression of Demetrios may have come from one of the issues in which he is depicted with an elephant scalp headdress, and perhaps more specifically from the pedigree coins of Agathokles where he is given the epithet *anikêtos* 'invincible'.

2.5 Early Modern Historical Studies

The 'first modern historian' of the Hellenistic Far East was the Sinologist Theophilus (Gottlieb) Siegfried Bayer, whose *Historia regni graecorum bactriani : in qua simul graecarum in India coloniarum vetus memoria* was published, on the basis of two Graeco-Bactrian coins and the Classical literary sources, in St. Petersburg in 1738 (Bayer 1738, available on Google Books). On Bayer's Sinological work and intellectual milieu, see Lundbæk 1986, with briefer references to the *Historia regni graecorum bactriani* and other numismatic works. Bayer's work and its reception is discussed in Coloru 2009, 33-40. It appears to have remained a go-to reference work on Bactria for some time: the article on Bactria in the 1835 *Penny Cyclopædia of the Society for the Diffusion of Useful Knowledge*, for example, cites Bayer in several places, to the apparent exlusion of any other modern historical sources (Penny Cyclopædia 1835)

2.6 Historical Fiction

Given the lack of historical data available on the Hellenistic Far East, it is not the most likely setting for an historical novel. Some examples, of varying quality in terms of historical accuracy and literary merit, include *Alexander at the World's End* (T. Holt 1999, the wryly humorous story of a reluctant Greek settler at Alexandria Eschate), *Horses of Heaven* (Bradshaw 1991, an historical romance about the marriage of a Graeco-Bactrian princess to a Saka king), and the Polish writer Teodor Parnicki's *Koniec Zgody Narodów: powieść z roku 179 przed narodzeniem Chrystusa*, with its interesting fictional prefiguration of the modern scholarly focus on cultural and genetic hybridity in Hellenistic Central Asia (translated into French as *La Fin de «L'Entente des peuples»*, Parnicki 1991; discussed in Jamroziak 1978). On Graeco-Bactrian kings in the science fiction of H. P. Lovecraft (as well as the medieval sources), see Coloru 2008.

Rudyard Kipling's story *The Man Who Would Be King* (1888) describes the attempt of two British soldiers to set themselves up as kings of a pagan tribe in the mountains of Kafiristan (present-day Nuristan in south-eastern Afghanistan). The members of this tribe are hinted to be descendents of the army of Alexander the Great – their fair complexions and European features are commented upon – and the soldiers initially succeed by representing themselves as gods and as descendents of Alexander. These themes are made more explicit in the 1975 film directed by John Huston (Section 2.7). The notion that any Greek cultural or genetic legacy may be traced among the peoples of Afghanistan is essentially fantasy – see e.g. the wishful thinking of Leeming 2003 – and has yet to be supported by any compelling historical or scientific evidence (see the most recent discussion of the genetic evidence in Firasat, et al. 2007).

2.7 Cinema

Most of the numerous films on the life and campaigns of Alexander the Great contain some depiction of what would become the Hellenistic Far East. For an interesting collection of critical essays on the latest such offering, Oliver Stone's *Alexander* (2004), including several on Persian and Central Asian matters, see Cartledge and Greenland 2010.

At least two Hindi films have been made about Alexander's campaigns in India. *Sikandar* (1941, dir. Sohrab Modi) was released during the Second World War and the Quit India campaign, and its depiction of the resistance of the Indian king Porus to the European invader Alexander is full of contemporary resonance (for a full discussion see Vasunia 2010; this film is available on YouTube, <youtube.com>, accessed 17 November 2010). *Sikandar-e-Azam* (1965, dir. Kedar Kapoor) again depicts the conflict and subsequent peace between Porus and Alexander. The actor Prithviraj Kapoor (1906-1972) appeared in both films, in the title role in *Sikandar*, and over twenty years later as Porus in *Sikandar-e-Azam*.

The 1975 film adaptation of *The Man Who Would Be King* (directed and adapted by John Huston, starring Michael Caine and Sean Connery) is more explicit in its references to Alexander and his supposed cultural and genetic legacy in Afghanistan than Kipling's original story. As well as the soldiers' claim to be sons of Alexander, the holy city of Kafiristan is called Sikandergul, and the local girl who reveals the Englishmen to be mortals is called Roxane.

CHAPTER 3
CULTURE AND IDENTITY IN THE HELLENISTIC FAR EAST

3.1 The Hellenistic Far East: Cultural Custody Battles

In the first volume of the series *Mémoires de la Délégation archéologique française en Afghanistan*, *La vieille route de l'Inde de Bactres à Taxila* (1942-47), Alfred Foucher was forced, with some regret, to dismiss the notion of a strong Greek culture in Hellenistic Bactria – gleaned from the Classical historical sources, and the impressive Greek numismatic record of the region – as a 'mirage'. Foucher's lengthy excavations at Balkh, ancient Bactra – eighteen months, under harsh climatic conditions - had failed to reveal any Greek monuments. The abundant Greek coinage of the region, he suggested, gave a misleading impression of the actual cultural dynamics of the Graeco-Bactrian and Indo-Greek states (Foucher and Bazin-Foucher 1942/47, 73-75, 310; see further Chapter 5, Section 5.1, below on the history of archaeological research in the Hellenistic Far East).

Foucher can hardly be faulted for his insistence that statements about the culture and society of the Hellenistic Far East be backed up with archaeological evidence. In his discussion of Classical influence in the later art and architecture of the region, however, Daniel Schlumberger, a subsequent Director of the DAFA, argued that this influence can only have arisen from a local tradition of Greek art and craftsmanship. In contrast to Foucher, he claimed that "la Bactriane n'est pas un mythe, elle est seulement inexplorée" (Schlumberger 1960, 152; cf. Schlumberger 1946). Schlumberger was vindicated by the discovery of the city of Ai Khanoum, which finally gave material substance to the *mirage bactrien*. The series which Foucher had inaugurated went on to publish dramatic finds of Greek architecture, artefacts and inscriptions from these excavations (on the 'Bactrian mirage' and the archaeological reality, see Kuz'mina 1976 and Holt 1987).

The wealth of new archaeological material which emerged from Central Asia during the 1960s and 1970s rapidly began to pose problems of its own. The complicated intersections of artistic and architectural styles at Ai Khanoum reveal no straightforward Greek-'Oriental' dichotomy. Hellenistic Bactria, it has been suggested, is not a mirage but a paradigm, a case-study where the diverse and problematic forms of evidence allow us to apply and test our ideas about the Hellenistic world (F. L. Holt 1999, 9-20). One of the key questions which emerges from any such analysis is that of how the material culture of the Hellenistic Far East relates to the society which created it.

It is tempting to divide the intellectual history of the Hellenistic Far East into 'Before Ai Khanoum' and 'After Ai Khanoum'. Ai Khanoum does indeed represent a turning-point of a sort, in that it was the first site to be excavated which was strikingly 'Greek' – something which Foucher had searched for in vain – but also because of the celebrity it achieved among the international scholarly community (see e.g. Paul Bernard's article in *Scientific American*: P. Bernard 1982). But even 'After Ai Khanoum' there is a high degree of similarity – or rather continuity – in the research questions asked of the body of historical, numismatic, archaeological and epigraphic evidence from the Hellenistic Far East. Questions of culture and identity – variously phrased – have long been dominant in directing research goals in the region.

'Before Ai Khanoum' the most significant debate on the cultural identities of the populations of the Hellenistic Far East was between W. W. Tarn and A. K. Narain. Tarn's *The Greeks in Bactria and India* (1st edition 1938) and Narain's *The Indo-Greeks* (1957) were reliant on the numismatic evidence from the region and on the limited reports in various Greek, Roman, Indian and Chinese historical sources. Tarn's view was that Bactria was the 'fifth Hellenistic state'. Narain's judgement on the Indo-Greeks was that "they came, they saw, but India conquered" (Narain 1957, 18).

This debate has arguably become more polarised (and, indeed, paradigmatic) than it was ever considered to be by the participants (see the discussion in Mairs 2006b; Narain 1992 provides a useful clarification of his position). Tarn was not necessarily arguing that the populations of the Hellenistic Far East were Greek, and Narain was not arguing that they were Indian. What they did do was to put their emphasis on different facets of the history of the region. Bactria, with its architectural traditions, use of the Greek language in public inscriptions and administration, and royal iconography was unquestionably a 'Hellenistic state'. 'Hellenistic', of course, does not mean the same thing as 'Greek'. A degree of cultural interaction or 'fusion' is implicit in the term. The various other Successor states of the Hellenistic East had much in common with contemporary Bactria, in terms of their diverse populations and the depth of the cultural and political engagement between Greek and non-Greek.

In terms of the ultimate political (and cultural) fate of the Indo-Greeks, Narain was also correct that ultimately "India conquered". By the early first century AD, Greek-named kings had ceased to issue coins in north-western India. Although 'assimilation' and 'acculturation' are terms which it is dangerous to use without more thorough consideration of the social processes at work (see further below), this is more or less what, in the end, happened to the Greek populations of the Hellenistic Far East. For an intially small settler population in a region far from their Aegean homeland, this is not so unpredictable a fate. What is interesting is the period of time – around three centuries – during which different cultural influences co-existed in the material culture of the Hellenistic Far East.

Much ('After Ai Khanoum') has since been written about the contact or 'fusion' of different traditions in the architecture and material culture of the Hellenistic Far East. In moving beyond the unproductive (and rather tedious) 'Greek versus Indian' debate, however, it is important not to fall, by default, into an equally unproductive mode of analysis: that of characterising the culture of the Hellenistic Far East as a lumpen, undifferentiated, 'fusion', without devoting sufficient attention to the agency of the populations who created, manipulated and lived with this 'fusion'. The following section will discuss some issues in postcolonial and archaeological theory which have the potential to offer productive approaches to the archaeological evidence from the Hellenistic Far East

3.2 Theory and Archaeological Practice

The discussion in this section, on theoretical approaches to the material culture and documentary evidence from the Hellenistic Far East, runs the risk of becoming rather dated, rather quickly. I have tried, as far as possible, not to jump too enthusiastically on theoretical bandwagons: for a healthy critique of seductive-yet-barren 'postmodernist babble', see Leo 1999; and for a critical discussion of 'identity' in the Hellenistic East, and Hellenistic Bactria more specifically, Mairs 2010a. My goal is to isolate a few key theoretical approaches (and demonstrate that such approaches can have productive, and sometimes unexpected results), not to argue for the validity of any one particular trope over another. Some of these constructs have already been influential in the analysis of material from the Hellenistic Far East, while others – culled from the wider world of social and archaeological theory – may yet produce interesting results.

My discussion and bibliographies are – for the obvious reason that I discuss theoretical approaches only in terms of their application to the Hellenistic Far East – less than comprehensive. The first section deals with the 'colonial' Hellenistic Far East, although much of the formulation of this model is 'post-colonial' in date. Certain of the following sections, especially Section 3.2.6. on the 'places in between', may be considered to constitute the 'postcolonial' Hellenistic Far East.

3.2.1 The Colonial Hellenistic Far East

The temptation to compare the campaigns of Alexander the Great, and Greek settlement in the Hellenistic Far East, with Early Modern and Modern European colonial activity in the region is difficult to resist. Most recently, the misadventures of the Soviet Union and the United States-led Coalition in Afghanistan have provoked various explorations of how and why the territories around the Hindu Kush have managed to resist major imperial powers so effectively (see e.g. Holt 2005).

In addition to the literary and cinematic representations of the region discussed in Chapter 2, Sections 2.6 and 2.7 (in particular Kipling's *The Man Who Would Be King*, whether in print or on screen, and the 1941 Hindi film *Sikandar*: Vasunia 2010), many treatments of the Hellenistic Far East contain passing references to or comparisons with British India (see e.g. several places in Green 1990). In part, this is a product of the 'colonial Indology' developed in the eighteenth and nineteenth centuries (Chakrabarti 1997). British administrators in India, almost always with Classical educations, constructed particular ways of viewing the Indian past. On views of the 'Hellenistic' presence in India in particular, see Mairs 2006b, and on wider questions of the Classics in the Raj, and the Raj in the Classics, Hall and Vasunia 2010. The articles in Bradley 2010 treat the relationship between imperialism and the Classics in the British Empire as a whole.

Colonial issues and analogies in the Hellenistic Far East may also be discussed alongside Will's classic study of the 'colonial anthropology' of the Hellenistic world (Will 1985, see also Bagnall 1997). Studies of Hellenistic Bactria which employ similar vocabularies of colonisation and exploitation include Bernard 1981 and Rapin 1990. These studies are post-colonial in an historical sense, and are reactions to the histories of European colonialism in Asia, Africa and the Americas. Approaches to the Hellenistic world which set themselves within more recent theoretical constructions of the postcolonial world will be discussed in some of the following sections.

3.2.2 Ethnicity

The topic of ethnicity reached its height of archaeological popularity in the mid-late 1990s, and has since largely fallen from favour (see e.g. Bilde, et al. 1992; Hall 1997; Jones 1998; Malkin 1998; Mitchell and Greatrex 2000; Malkin 2001 – the latter from colloquia held some time previously). It has been raised, problematised, and largely dismissed in favour of postcolonial constructs such as hybridity, creolisation and so forth. The reasons for the decline and fall of ethnicity in archaeology are essentially: a) that it was always used in different ways by different people, and that the use of this common vocabulary for disparate concepts became intensely frustrating; b) that, despite the perspective granted by thorough historiographical studies such as Jones 1998, it continued to be understood by many in a primordialist sense; and c) that, like most theoretical constructs, it provides a constructive approach to some case studies but not to others. Ethnicity's irrelevance and, indeed, its potential to obfuscate in many such contexts unfortunately served to invalidate it more generally in archaeological discourse.

The archaeology of the Hellenistic Far East is, I would argue, one of those case studies in which 'ethnicity' does provide a useful way of understanding the social and cultural processes which produced our material record. This is something which I have argued repeatedly – perhaps to the point of monotony - in my own research, and I remain persuaded that to speak of ethnicity in discussing topics such as Central Asian funerary practice (Mairs 2007b) and the urban layout of Ai Khanoum

(Mairs forthcoming-b) is a useful thing to do (see also Mairs 2008 and the unpublished thesis Mairs 2006a).

I define 'ethnicity' in a slightly old-fashioned, but I believe still very valid, sense: as a 'constructed' identity, predicated upon the selective mobilisation of aspects of cultural behaviour and material culture in the construction of a group identity, in which the delineation of a 'boundary' between one's own group and others is an essential part of the process. This is more-or-less the definition of ethnicity and ethnic behaviour already established in Barth 1969. What is important in the construction of an ethnic group and the maintenance of its boundaries is not that a group have any objective common 'culture', but that they take aspects of their cultural toolkit and invest them with ethnic significance. It is therefore impossible to identify an ethnic group, in this sense, in terms of observable behaviour such as language use, or material culture such as dress, ceramic forms, or architecture. It is also difficult, in the archaeological record, to identify what forms of material culture are being used 'ethnically' and which are not.

This is the essential problem on which key works archaeological studies of ethnicity such as Jones 1998 unfortunately failed to convince. The challenge is to provide a case study which shows that we *can* identify ethnic behaviour in the archaeological record. One of the best such examples of which I am aware, and which explicitly sets itself this challenge, is S. T. Smith's study of the New Kingdom Egyptian empire in Nubia (Smith 2003). This work, among other things, contrasts indigenous culinary practice within domestic contexts with the self-conscious Egyptianising of funerary architecture among the colonial population. It is the examination of multiple arenas of human activity, such as this, which may allow us to see what forms of behaviour and public display are considered to impact on a group's projected identity and which are not. At Ai Khanoum, I have argued that 'indigenous' or 'Mesopotamian' religious activity was not thought to compromise communal Greek cultural and civic identity, however striking such activity may appear in the material record (Mairs 2008; Mairs forthcoming-b, the more detailed study was written in 2005, and is available online at <http://oxford.academia.edu/RachelMairs/Papers>, accessed 11 January 2011).

Other potential case studies could be examined. Although there is not sufficient material from domestic contexts at any site in the Hellenistic Far East to explore culinary practice, the commodities contained in vessels from places such as the Ai Khanoum Treasury (Chapter 5, Section 5.2.2 and Chapter 6, Section 6.2.3.1) might allow us to consider evidence for the importation – or even production – of olive oil alongside Strabo's (II 1.14) oft-quoted lament that Central Asia does not grow olives, the archetypal 'Greek' agricultural product and an implicit index of Hellenicity.

3.2.3 Movement of Objects and Transformations in Meaning

The notion that the relationship between an object and its meaning may change (see e.g. Kopytoff 1986; Gosden and Marshall 1999) has important implications for our understanding of long-distance movement of material culture and stylistic traits in the Hellenistic Far East. A Corinthian column at Ai Khanoum (Paul Bernard 1968), simply put, may not have the same cultural associations to an inhabitant of that city as to a contemporary inhabitant of a Greek city of the Mediterranean littoral, or, indeed, to a modern analyst. Familiar forms and motifs can be deconstructed and reimagined in different ways in different contexts: take, for example, the terracotta 'assembled' Corinthian capitals from Parthian Nisa (Invernizzi 1995a).

A useful case study – informative because we can trace the routes along which these objects moved in some detail – is the presence of small beads and amulets from Roman Egypt in post-Graeco-Bactrian Central Asia (Rtveladze 1977; Sherkova 1981; Mairs 2007a). It is unlikely that these reflect any direct link with Egypt, still less any perception that these items were 'Egyptian' in any meaningful sense. The contexts in which these items occur reveal how their associations changed along their route, from the Black Sea across the steppes, between Egypt and Central Asia. In the northern Black Sea littoral, they occur in the graves of children; in Central Asia, in the graves of women. In both regions, as in their original Egyptian context, such amulets have an evident association with fertility and the protection of women and children. But the precise meaning they are given is different in different places.

In many cases, we can do little more than pose the question of whether items and styles 'imported' into the Hellenistic Far East from the Mediterranean world, Central Asia or South Asia have the same purpose and cultural associations as they do in their context of production or formulation. The example of the 'Mesopotamian' temple at Ai Khanoum was discussed above. We might ask similar questions of the 'Greek' elements in the Ai Khanoum cityscape, which have of course been frequently discussed, but have not been problematised to the same extent as the 'non-Greek' elements. The fountain spout in the shape of a comic mask, and the literary and dramatic papyri from the Treasury, give the theatre, at least some wider local cultural context. This was a theatre in a familiar Greek form, with at least some of the usual trappings – masks and Greek plays – of Greek dramatic performance. But how might the theatre's performers and clientele have reimagined the dramatic arts in eastern Bactria?

Another way of disentangling objects and styles from their cultural associations in the Hellenistic Far East is to look at mechanisms of transmission. The opportunities to do so are limited, but have the potential to yield interesting results. The plaster medallions from the Kushan-period storerooms at Begram (Menninger 1996) are an excellent illustration of how images might be not just imitated, but precisely reproduced, over long distances. These medallions, which depict very 'Classical' figures and imagery, are very small – at most, a little over 20 cm in diameter – and thus very portable. They are moulds taken from metal vessels, upon which reproductions can be modelled. Finished objects might themselves be transported between the Mediterranean and Central Asia, but the mechanisms of reproduction might also be transported, without the movement of bulkier or more fragile pieces.

Participation in common bureaucratic systems meant that the language, palaeography and formulae of the Aramaic and Greek administrative documents from Achaemenid and Hellenistic Bactria were all but identical to examples from contemporary Egypt. This question will be discussed further below.

3.2.4 Space and Landscape

One of the most interesting developments in Central Asian archaeology in the past couple of decades has been the increasing use of archaeological field survey techniques to reveal ancient patterns of land usage and exploitation, and the relationship between urban settlements and their agricultural hinterlands. The most significant of these are the eastern Bactria survey, carried out during the 1970s, but only published in its final form in the 1990s (Chapter 5, Section 5.2.2: Hinterland), and the Surkhan-darya valley survey projects (Chapter 5, Section 5.2.4: The Surkhan-darya – Survey and GIS). Work in the Murghab Delta, around the city of Merv, should also be noted, but material of the Achaemenid and Hellenistic periods is still poorly represented there (Chapter 5, Section 5.2.9).

It is likely to be some years before sufficient information on the urban layout of cities such as Bactra, Kandahar and Samarkand becomes available to address issues of space and access, but even at Ai Khanoum such questions largely remain to be explored. J.-C. Liger's 1979 *Maîtrise* thesis *La physionomie urbaine d'une cité hellénistique en Asie Centrale* unfortunately remains upublished (Liger 1979: Université de Paris VIII, Département d'Urbanisme; see also Mairs forthcoming-b).

3.2.5 Places in Between: The Postcolonial Hellenistic Far East

Another problem with (perceived) earlier scholarly debates between 'Greek' and 'Indian' influence on the culture of the Hellenistic Far East is that they treat cultures as reified, bounded units, corporate entitites which act in unison and may be isolated in our analysis. The postcolonial theoretical vocabulary for the spaces of interaction and negotiation between traditionally-defined 'cultures' has, however, been enthusiastically taken up by archaeologists and historians of the Hellenistic world. The Hellenistic Far East is as good a testing-ground as any for exploring how such theoretical concepts may – or may not – help us towards a better understanding of the ethnic and cultural dynamics of the region. Young 2001 provides, in general, an accessible and comprehensive introduction to the postcolonial world and how it has shaped and been shaped by various political and cultural theories.

The origins of such vocabulary may be taken from modern colonial contexts (*mestizo/mestizaje*, creolisation), biology (hybridity) or the geographical arenas of cultural contact (the middle ground). The point should be made that these terms are 'taken': these concepts often evolve considerably in the course of their adaptation to new historical and disciplinary contexts. Such adaptation, 'creative misunderstandings' analogous to transformations of meaning of cultural forms in the historical contexts themselves (Deloria 2006), are often very productive. But it should be recognised that the theoretical evolution has taken place, and that this evolution is sometimes necessary in order for the terminology or concept to have any applicability to archaeological evidence at all.

A good example of this is the concept of 'hybridity'. It is *de rigeur* to make reference to Homi Bhabha's *The Location of Culture* (Bhabha 1994), but archaeological interpretations and applications of the term have a rather indirect relationship to Bhabha's work of literary theory. The style in which *The Location of Culture* is written also makes it extremely difficult to extract clear points or individual strands of argument, and anecdotal and published evidence (e.g. Leo 1999) suggests that few archaeologists or Classicists who read it get much concrete useful material from the book itself. For a lucid discussion of hybridity, and the strengths and historical implications of Bhabha's work, see Young 1995.

As well as the indirectness of the relationship between archaeological theories or hybridity and their supposed source in the work of Bhabha and other scholars, there are also ways in which 'hybridity' in its postcolonial sense may not transfer well to historical contexts before modern European colonial enterprises. In particular, there is a potential clash between postcolonial hybridity's active and self-conscious negotiation between cultures, and the formation of new identities, and the efforts we may observe in some populations of the Hellenistic Far East to defend monolithic 'old' identities. Hybridity may therefore present a useful trope in analysing the material culture of the Hellenistic Far East, but it may well have been a concept which was entirely alien to the cultural outlook of the people who created and used this material culture. The choice to call something 'hybrid' is ours (Colonial Latin America: Dean and Leibsohn 2003; HFE: Mairs 2010b).

Other such concepts, although they can generate productive approaches to our evidence, also require to be situated historically. Richard White's 'middle ground', for example, originated as a literal description of a geographical territory in which native Americans and European settlers interacted, and by metaphorical extension to the creative cultural dialogue instigated in this liminal space (White 1991). The middle ground's further metaphorical extension to refer to zones of cultural interaction in general was not something intended in

White's original thesis, but this fact does not discredit the uses to which it has been put in other historical contexts (Deloria 2006). The point, once again, is that theoretical evolution and reinterpretation does not invalidate a concept, where it is found to be useful or evocative in ways beyond its original formulation. Tracing this evolution may, however, be extremely useful in allowing us to identify which aspects of the theory in question are historically contingent.

The archaeology of the Hellenistic Far East has thus far attracted only very limited analysis in the kinds of postcolonial theoretical veins outlined above. Instigating such analysis ought to be an important part of bringing the region into closer dialogue with scholarship on other regions of the Hellenistic world, and, indeed, neighbouring regions of South and East Asia. The essays in Canepa 2010 provide a useful demonstration of the various uses to which theories of cultural interaction may be put in a Eurasian context.

3.2.6 Multilingualism and Administration

Although the corpus of textual material in any one language (Aramaic, Greek, Bactrian) from Central Asia in the latter part of the first millennium BC and early centuries AD is relatively small, there is greater potential for research into linguistic questions than has hitherto been realised. The textual material discussed here is outlined, with further references, in Chapter 6. Consideration of the Aramaic, Greek and Bactrian material in conjunction offers the opportunity to look at changes and continuities in language use and administrative practices within Central Asia over time. And consideration of the material in any one of these languages alongside contemporary documents from the wider Achaemenid or Hellenistic empires reveals the extent to which Bactria and Arachosia were integrated into wider imperial administrative structures.

Administering Bactria, from the Achaemenids to the Kushans

The new Aramaic documentary texts from Bactria (Shaked 2004) have a key role to play in addressing both of these questions. First of all, they allow us to say something – even if not much – about administrative practice in Bactria from the Achaemenids through to the Kushans (to be discussed in Mairs forthcoming-a). The Aramaic, Greek and Bactrian administrative texts are small in number and separated by great distances in time, and possibly space (since their findspots are often unknown). But they do allow us to cautiously put forward a few hypotheses. One is about the retention of administrative personnel and administrative practices through regime change. The Aramaic documents cover the period of the collapse of the Persian Empire, and one, at least, of them has already begun to date by a regnal year of Alexander the Great. The adaptation of the Greek alphabet to write the Bactrian language, and certain pieces of evidence that some personnel were still able to write Greek in the second century AD (Chapter 6, Section 6.4.3), demonstrate the use to which the Kushans put Greek literacy and Greek literates in the administration of their own empire. There are also similarities in the form and medium (skin and long, narrow wooden slips) of Achaemenid, Graeco-Bactrian or Kushan documents.

Language and Politics

The epigraphic Greek of Central Asia is very self-consciously literary, far from any colloquial language, and it is difficult not to interpret it as an overt display of 'Greekness'. Was the Greek language, even before the fall of the Graeco-Bactrian and Indo-Greek kingdoms, already moribund? Bactrian, despite its Greek script, contains hardly any Greek loanwords. This suggests either (or both) that Greek had had little or no lasting impact on the spoken language(s) of Bactria, and that a deliberate policy of linguistic and political de-Hellenisation was implemented by the Kushan kings, and in particular Kanishka (Chapter 6, Section 6.4.3). The use of a written register was always, in some sense, a political act in Central Asia throughout this period. Whatever local languages were being spoken, there was usually only one available written language in which a person might erect an inscription or deal with the authorities. Short of devising a new way to record an oral language in writing – as happened under the Kushans – no written linguistic choice might be exercised. These various written languages, Aramaic, Greek or Bactrian, were to some extent standardised: loanwords were not introduced, or deliberately excluded, and forms of expression and stylistic conventions, whether bureaucratic formulae or overt literary sophistication, maintained. In Central Asia, it seems possible that there was a longstanding diglossic relationship between the language of writing, and of political and cultural authority, and the languages of everyday communication.

Achaemenid and Hellenistic Bureaucracies

As well as diachronic continuities within the Central Asian documentary context, the extant documents may also be used to explore long-distance geographical connections. They reveal in particular the extent to which Bactria must be considered as bureaucratically part of the empire of the Achaemenids, and of Alexander and his Successors, whatever the region's subsequent autonomy. As was suggested above, all the written languages of Achaemenid, Hellenistic and Kushan Central Asia are languages of political power. With the exception of Bactrian, they were probably not widely spoken as a first language at any point in the history of Central Asia. Neither the Imperial Aramaic nor the documentary Greek of Central Asia, however, are visibly influenced by any eastern Iranian oral substrate.

The documents from the Achaemenid-Hellenistic Far East are, on the other hand, very close in language, palaeography and structure to contemporary administrative documents from other regions of the empires in question. They are demonstrably products of Achaemenid and Hellenistic bureaucratic practice.

In both cases, documents from Egypt offer the most fruitful and striking comparanda: the many archives of third-century BC Egypt, such as that of Zenon (Pestman 1981); and the fifth-century Arshama documents (Driver 1957), to which Naveh and Shaked make reference in their forthcoming edition (Naveh and Shaked forthcoming). Egyptian and Bactrian hands, in both Aramaic and Greek, are all but identical, the product of the same broad schools of scribal training. The Aramaic documents of Egypt and of Bactria are written mostly on skin. In Egypt, at least, this is a deliberate departure from the preferred local writing medium, papyrus, but it should also be noted that the Aramaic documents found in Egypt were for the most part written elsewhere. The majority of Iranian loanwords in the Bactrian Aramaic documents are Old Persian in origin, and occur also in Aramaic texts of Egypt and the Near East. Bactrian Aramaic and Bactrian Greek – inasmuch as they exist as distinct registers at all – are the products of a vast Near Eastern administrative system, the essential mechanisms, and, indeed, hierarchies and professional training, of which remained in operation throughout the second half of the first millennium BC.

In Arachosia, we can even find a hint that the same kind of multilingual administration was in operation as in other provinces of the Achaemenid Empire. The use of Aramaic may be inferred indirectly, both from third-century inscriptions at Kandahar and in the Laghman Valley, and from the fourth-century Aramaic documents of neighbouring Bactria. It is the presence of Elamite, however, which is truly telling. A couple of fragments of a tablet of the same sort as were kept in the archives at Persepolis (Hallock 1969) were discovered at Kandahar. It therefore seems likely that the Achaemenid administration in Arachosia and Bactria observed the same functional differentiation between languages as in other regions of the empire (for further discussion of this question, see Briant, et al. 2008).

CHAPTER 4
GENERAL PUBLICATIONS

4.1 Introduction

The following chapters will cover the major thematic or site-specific publications on the Hellenistic Far East. I begin here with an inventory of some synthetic studies, edited volumes and catalogues which collect material on diverse subjects, sites or periods, or provide a wider conspectus of the region, its archaeology and history.

A section towards the end of this chapter will provide a basic 'starting-point' bibliography on a topic which falls outside the scope of this survey – the numismatic evidence from the Hellenistic Far East – which it would be irresponsible of me to attempt to cover fully.

4.2 Synthetic Historical Studies

Although the works of Tarn (*The Greeks in Bactria and India*, 1st ed. Cambridge 1938; subsequent editions Cambridge 1951 and Chicago 1985) and Narain (*The Indo-Greeks*, 1st edition Oxford 1957; revised edition Delhi 1980) are the traditional starting point – bibliographical and rhetorical – for research on the history of the Hellenistic Far East, it is difficult to recommend either as an accessible introduction. This is not just because they were written before the major archaeological excavations at Ai Khanoum and other Central Asian sites from the 1960s onwards, and were written with particular scholarly agendas (discussed in Mairs 2006b, and above, Chapter 3, Section 3.1), but also because our numismatic data-sets have grown and their evaluation advanced significantly.

Two recent books, by O. Coloru and F. Widemann, are likely to become new standard reference works. The approach of both is primarily historical and their major sources textual and numismatic, although both also take good account of the archaeological data.

Da Alessandro a Menandro: il regno greco di Battriana (Coloru 2009), in the series *Studi ellenistici*, covers both the history of the Hellenistic Far East and its reception in antiquity through to the present day (see also Chapter 2, Section 2.6 on the HFE in fiction). As it may not yet be available in many libraries, it should be noted that this work is summarised at some length and reviewed very positively by F. Canali De Rossi in the *Bryn Mawr Classical Review* 2010.10.33 (<http://bmcr.brynmawr.edu/2010/2010-10-33.html>, accessed 17 November 2010). The doctoral thesis from which the book evolved – although its published form is substantially different – may be downloaded as PDF files from the *Electronic Theses and Dissertations* databank of the Università di Pisa (<http://etd.adm.unipi.it/>, accessed 17 November 2010).

Les successeurs d'Alexandre en Asie centrale et leur héritage culturel. Essai. (Widemann 2009) is more numismatic in focus, and attempts the first comprehensive modern synthesis of the numismatic evidence on the Graeco-Bactrian and Indo-Greek kings, their dates and territorial possessions. It is, again, likely to set a benchmark in historical studies of the Hellenistic Far East. Widemann 2001, an earlier study, traces the history of Greek settlement in the East from the Achaemenids through to the end of Indo-Greek dominance.

Several books on Bactria by F. L. Holt should also be noted, in particular *Alexander the Great and Bactria: The Formation of a Greek Frontier in Central Asia* (Holt 1988) on Alexander and the Macedonian settlement of Bactria, and *Thundering Zeus: The Making of Hellenistic Bactria* (F. L. Holt 1999) on Bactria in the third century BC. *Alexander the Great and the Mystery of the Elephant Medallions* (Holt 2003) and *Into the Land of Bones: Alexander the Great in Afghanistan* (Holt 2005) may also be recommended for a more popular introduction to the history of Hellenistic Bactria, alongside numismatic case studies and the history of more recent wars in region.

There are a number of studies on individual episodes in the history of the Hellenistic Far East in the period of transition, from the late fourth to mid-third centuries BC, between Alexander's conquests and settlements, the establishment of Seleucid and Mauryan control, and the independence of Bactria-Sogdiana. Schober 1981, 89-93 and 140-193, discusses the easternmost satrapies of the former Achaemenid Empire from their conquest by Alexander through to Seleukos I's treaty with Chandragupta Maurya at the end of the fourth century. The identification of a number of 'Alexandrias' in the region is discussed by Paul Bernard 1982b; Numan N. Negmatov 1986; Leriche 2002; Rtweladse 2009; and various sections of Fraser 1996. In addition to Holt's works, the political upheavals of the third century BC, and Bactria's independence from the Seleucid Empire, are covered in Lerner 1999 and Bopearachchi 1994.

The UNESCO volume, *History of the Civilizations of Central Asia. Vol. 2, The Development of Sedentary and Nomadic Civilizations: 700 B.C. to A.D. 250* (Harmatta, Puri and Etemadi 1994) sets the Hellenistic Far East in its wider historical and geographical context. It also contains chapters on Central Asia under the Achaemenids and Kushans.

The following works on the Seleucid Empire also contain useful material on the Hellenistic Far East, in particular with regard to its relations with the other Hellenistic states:

- Kuhrt and Sherwin-White 1987: *Hellenism in the East: The interaction of Greek and non-Greek* civilizations from Syria to Central Asia after Alexander.

- Sherwin-White and Kuhrt 1993: *From Samarkhand to Sardis: A new approach to the Seleucid empire.*

4.3 Edited Volumes

Most of the volumes listed here are the proceedings of conferences or colloquia, not all devoted solely to material of the Achaemenid, Hellenistic and Kushan periods. Those representing the outcomes of collaboration between French and Soviet scholars are of particular interest.

- Deshayes 1977: *Le Plateau iranien et l'Asie Centrale des origines à la conquête islamique : leurs relations à la lumière des documents archéologiques, Paris 22-24 mars 1976.*

- Asimov et al. 1985: *L'archéologie de la Bactriane ancienne. Actes du Colloque franco-soviétique, Dushanbe (U.R.S.S.), 27 octobre – 3 novembre 1982.*

- Leriche and Tréziny 1986: *La fortification dans l'histoire du monde grec : actes du Colloque international La Fortification et sa place dans l'histoire politique, culturelle et sociale du monde grec, Valbonne, décembre 1982.*

- Grenet 1987b: *Cultes et monuments religieux dans l'Asie centrale préislamique.*

- Francfort 1990: *Nomades et sédentaires en Asie centrale: Apports de l'archéologie et de l'ethnologie. Actes du Colloque franco-soviétique Alma Ata (Kazakhstan) 17-26 octobre 1987.*

- Bernard and Grenet 1991: *Histoire et cultes de l'Asie centrale préislamique: Sources écrites et documents archéologiques. Actes du colloque international du CNRS (Paris, 22-28 Novembre 1988).*

- Errington and Cribb 1992: *The Crossroads of Asia: Transformation in Image and Symbol in the Art of Ancient Afghanistan and Pakistan.*

- Invernizzi 1995b: *In the Land of the Gryphons: Papers on Central Asian Archaeology in Antiquity.*

- A special volume of the *Bulletin of the Asia Institute* (Vol. 12, 1998): *Alexander's Legacy in the East: Studies in Honor of Paul Bernard.*

- Leriche, et al. 2001: *La Bactriane au carrefour des routes et des civilisations de l'Asie centrale: Termez et les villes de Bactriane-Tokharestan: Actes du colloque de Termez 1997.*

- Bopearachchi and Boussac 2005: *Afghanistan. Ancien carrefour entre l'est et l'ouest. Actes du colloque international au Musée archéologique Henri-Prades-Lattes du 5 au 7 mai 2003.*

- Cribb and Herrmann 2007: *After Alexander: Central Asia Before Islam.*

- Abdullaev 2010: Традиции Востока и Запада в Античной Культуре Средней Азии: Сборник Статей в Честь Поля Бернара - *The Traditions of East and West in the Antique Cultures of Central Asia: Papers in Honor of Paul Bernard.*
A table of contents, in Russian and French/English, for this Paul Bernard Festschrift is available online at <http://claude.rapin.free.fr/Paul%20Bernard%20sbornik2%20-%20Rapin.pdf> (accessed 9 January 2011), along with the full text of one article, Rapin 2010. The full volume was unfortunately not available to me.

4.4 Exhibition Catalogues

4.4.1 The National Museum, Kabul

A wonderful resource on the pre-war collections of the National Museum of Afghanistan, Kabul is available in Tissot 2006, *Catalogue of the National Museum of Afghanistan, 1931-1985*, compiled from photographs taken by visitors to the Museum over a period of some decades (see also Tissot 2002). Dupree, et al. 1974, *The National Museum of Afghanistan: An Illustrated Guide* (replacing two earlier editions), and Rowland 1971, *Art in Afghanistan: Objects from the Kabul Museum*, are earlier catalogues of the collection.

Sarianidi 1985, *Bactrian Gold: From the Excavations of the Tillya-Tepe Necropolis in Northern Afghanistan*, is a well-illustrated 'coffee-table book' of the finds from the post-Graeco-Bactrian tombs at Tillya Tepe in Bactria, which survived the war in Kabul, and have more recently been part of a major touring exhibition in Europe and North America (see further below).

4.4.2 Loans from the National Museum, Kabul

- [...] 1963: *Afuganisutan kodai Bijutsuten – Exhibition of Ancient Art of Afghanistan.* (Tokyo, Nihonbashi Takashimaya: 3 Sept. – 15 Sept., 1963; Osaka, Namba Takashimaya: 24 Sept. – 6 Oct., 1963; Nagoya, Sakae-cho Maruei Department Store Co. Ltd.: 19 Oct. – 30 Oct., 1963.)

- Rowland 1966: *Ancient Art from Afghanistan: Treasures of the Kabul Museum.* (Asia House Gallery, New York City: 13 Jan. – 6 Mar., 1966; The Los Angeles County Museum of Art, Lytton Gallery: 25 Mar. – 16 May, 1966; National Collection of Fine Arts, Smithsonian Institution, Washington D.C.: 29 June – 23 Aug., 1966.)

- Royal Academy of Arts [1967]: *Ancient Art from Afghanistan, at the Royal Academy of Arts, 6 December 1967 to 28 January 1968.*

- Cambon and Jarrige 2006: *Afghanistan, les trésors retrouvés: Collections du musée national de Kaboul, Musee Guimet, 6 décembre 2006 au 30 avril 2007.* (Educational website on the exhibition: <http://www.guimet.fr/tresorsafghans/index.html>, accessed 15 November 2010.)

- Hiebert and Cambon 2008: *Afghanistan: Hidden Treasures from the National Museum, Kabul.* (National Gallery of Art, Washington, D.C. 25 May – 7 Sept., 2008; Asian Art Museum of San Francisco, 24 Oct., 2008 – 25 Jan., 2009; The Museum of Fine Arts, Houston, 1 Mar. – 17 May, 2009; The Metropolitan Museum of Art, New York, 23 June – 20 Sept., 2009; Canadian Museum of Civilization, Gatineau-Ottawa, 23 Oct., 2009 – 28 Mar., 2010; Bonn Museum, 11 June, 2010 – 2 Jan., 2011; British Museum, London, 3 Mar. – 3 July 2011) (Website: <http://www.nationalgeographic.com/mission/afghanistan-treasures/>, accessed 15 November 2010.)

4.4.3 Other Exhibitions of Central Asian Material

- Miho Museum 2002: *Treasures of Ancient Bactria. Catalog of an exhibition held at the Miho Museum, Aug. 18 –Sept. 1 2002.*

- Bopearachchi, et al. 2003: *De l'Indus à l'Oxus: Archéologie de l'Asie centrale. Catalogue de l'exposition* (Musée de Lattes). The accompanying volume of papers, Bopearachchi and Boussac 2005: *Afghanistan: Ancien carrefour entre l'est et l'ouest*, is noted above.

- Reiss-Engelhorn-Museen 2009: *Alexander der Grosse und die Öffnung der Welt : Asiens Kulturen im Wandel* (Reiss-Engelhorn-Museen, Mannheim 3 Oct., 2009 - 21 Feb., 2010).

4.5 Numismatics

Despite its important role in studies of the political and cultural history of the Hellenistic Far East, I will not provide any thorough presentation or discussion of numismatic evidence here. This is not only because the focus of this survey is primarily archaeological, but also because I simply do not possess the necessary numismatic expertise. I limit myself to citing a few of the more general or accessible surveys, through which further bibliography and more in-depth discussion may be followed up.

The earliest modern European historical work on the Hellenistic Far East, Bayer's *Historia regni graecorum bactriani* (Bayer 1738) discussed Graeco-Bactrian coins in St. Petersburg alongside the scanty Classical historical sources (See Chapter 2, Section 2.5, above for further references). Bopearachchi 2007 discusses Alfred Foucher and numismatic studies in the early years of the DAFA. Some of the most important recent numismatic finds in the region, often compromised by their lack of secure provenance, are treated in Bopearachchi 2002 and Bopearachchi and Flandrin 2005. The most recent 'numismatic history' of the Hellenistic Far East is that of Widemann 2009.

The majority of the Greek kings of the Hellenistic Far East are known only from their coinage. Careful study of monograms, die sequences and overstrikes can produce invaluable evidence on relative chronology and territorial possessions (see, e.g., the work of Bopearachchi 1991a, Senior and MacDonald 1998, Kritt 2001, or Cribb 2005), but much is open to interpretation. There has sometimes been a dangerous tendency for speculation to be presented as fact: see the somewhat pessimistic discussion in Seldeslachts 2004. Further methodological issues are presented in Guillaume 1990 and Guillaume 1991. Wider economic and financial questions arising from the numismatic evidence are addressed in, e.g., Bernard 1979 and Rtveladze 1984a.

The most compendious publications of Graeco-Bactrian and Indo-Greek coins are O. Bopearachchi's catalogues of the collection of the Bibliothèque nationale in Paris (Bopearachchi 1991b), the Smithsonian Institution in Washington, D.C. (Bopearachchi 1993), and the American Numismatic Society (Bopearachchi 1998), which also contain wider discussion, and draw up proposed chronologies.

Coins from individual archaeological sites will be discussed where relevant in the appropriate sections of Chapter 5.

CHAPTER 5
ARCHAEOLOGY

5.1 Introduction

5.1.1 History of Archaeological Research

The foundation and subsequent history of the *Délégation archéologique française en Afghanistan* has been the subject of a book-length treatment by F. Olivier-Utard, who sets the DAFA in its wider political context, as an organ of the French Ministry of Foreign Affairs (Olivier-Utard 1997). The latter part of this work, concerning many scholars who are still alive and active in the field, has been reviewed critically by Grenet 1999. Paul Bernard 2002 also discusses the first incarnation of the DAFA from its foundation in 1922 through to its dissolution in 1982.

For contemporary accounts of archaeological research in Soviet Central Asia, see Masson 1966 (German translation: Masson 1982), as well as Frumkin 1970 and the relevant chapters of Mongait 1961. The discussion of the theoretical principles and methodological procedures of Soviet archaeology in Bulkin, et al. 1982 is also useful.

Gorshenina and Rapin 2001 is a popular, and well-illustrated, overview of archaeological research in Central Asia as a whole. On the history of archaeological fieldwork in southern Uzbekistan, in the valley of the Surkhan-darya and at Termez, see Pougatchenkova 2001b and Pougatchenkova 2001a (a personal account).

For accounts of the work of French archaeological missions in Central Asia to 2000, see the report in *Cahiers d'Asie centrale* 9 (2001). This includes reports on the Mission Archéologique Franco-Ouzbèke (MAFOUZ: 1989 onwards, esp. Afrasiab and Kok-tepe) (Grenet and Isamiddinov 2001); Mission Archéologique Franco-Ouzbèque de Bactriane (MAFOUZ de Bactriane: 1993 onwards, regional survey and excavation) (Leriche and Pidaev 2001); and on the Mission Archéologique Française en Asie centrale (MAFAC: set up in 1982 after closure of the DAFA) (Francfort 2001). For a breakdown of the sites and personnel of the MAFAC, see Francfort 1993. Besenval 2001 discusses Franco-Tajik cooperation.

A bibliography of Paul Bernard's publications 1959-1999 is given in the *Bulletin of the Asia Institute* 12, 1998, 3-11. Several titles and other details are incorrect and some may be 'ghosts'.

5.1.2 Problems and Methodologies

The amount of archaeological material available for study from the Hellenistic Far East, whether excavated or bought and sold on the antiquities market, has increased steadily over the past few decades, as has the accompanying corpus of scholarly publications. But there are still some notable, and highly problematic, archaeological lancunae. The comparative lack of excavation at Bactra, at least until recent years, has inevitably skewed our impressions of other Bactrian urban sites. At Ai Khanoum, for example, our choice to describe the city's central complex of buildings as a 'palace' or 'administrative quarter' depends on what we consider the political status of the city as a whole to have been. If and when the Hellenistic levels at Bactra are more thoroughly excavated, it will be possible to recontextualise Ai Khanoum. At Takht-i Sangin, excavation has been largely confined to the citadel, and it is still difficult to gain much sense of the wider settlement beyond the central temple complex.

Many of the major urban settlements in Central Asia (Merv, Samarkand, Termez, Bactra, etc.) remained in constant occupation over extremely long periods. All of the latter were only relocated and rebuilt on adjacent sites after their destruction by the Mongols in AD 1220-1221. The archaeologist is therefore presented with some vast and formidable tell sites, where the Hellenistic-period strata are often buried under over a thousand years' worth of subsequent occupation levels. Merv (Section 5.2.9) is unlikely to reveal its Hellenistic or Hellenistic-contemporary levels any time in the near future. On the other hand, multi-period sites and survey projects provide an opportunity to view settlement and land-use in the region over the longue durée. The field-survey projects in eastern Bactria (Section 5.2.2: Hinterland), the Surkhan-darya Valley (Section 5.2.4) and the Murghab Delta (Section 5.2.9) enable us to contextualise the small amount of data from the Achaemenid, Hellenistic and Kushan periods within a much larger body of material from the Bronze Age through into the Islamic period.

5.1.3 Research Tools and Thematic Studies

The following section will present the archaeological material from the Hellenistic Far East by region, and within this by archaeological site or survey area. This is not, however, a gazetteer of the sort compiled by Ball and Gardin for Afghanistan (Ball 1982; see also Gardin 1982: the integration of this work and other data from Afghanistan into an archaeological GIS database is signalled in Padwa 2004, although I have been unable to find any more recent information on the progress of this project). A large number of the sites identified as having Achaemenid, Hellenistic or Kushan levels in Ball's Gazetteer (see the chronological index to Vol. II and the thematic bibliographies, especially Section 4.14) were subject to only very brief inspections, and have little or no additional bibliography. The only data available on such sites, which may not have survived the thirty years of war since the Gazetteer's publication, are brief mentions in broader or more general publications. The sites I discuss in the following sections, in Afghanistan, and the Hellenistic Far East as a whole, are those for which we have at least some published archaeological data.

A number of studies discusss individual features and aspects of the archaeology of the Hellenistic Far East on a regional level. The excavated temples and other religious structures of Hellenistic Bactria have received the most intensive analyses, and are the subject of studies by Bernard 1990b; Boyce and Grenet 1991, 165–179; and, in conjunction with the Seleucid evidence, Downey 1988 and Hannestad and Potts 1990. Litvinskii and Pichikyan 2000, 283-293, explicitly consider the Temple of the Oxus at Takht-i Sangin alongside Ai Khanoum and Dil'berdzhin.

The archaeological evidence for funerary practice in Hellenistic Bactria is assessed in the relevant sections of Grenet 1984 (which covers Central Asia as a whole across all periods from the Graeco-Macedonian conquest to the rise of Islam) and, in conjunction with questions of ethnic identity, Mairs 2007b. Litvinskii and Sedov 1984 cover the funerary material from Kushan Bactria.

Fortifications are treated in Francfort 1979 (another study with a broader chronological and geographical scope); and in various articles (Pougatchenkova 1986 covers several Central Asian sites), and group discussion ([Collectif] 1986) published in Leriche and Tréziny 1986. As well as site- or region-specific articles, there are also those which treat Central Asian fortifications in terms of their possible connections with the Near East and Mediterranean world (Kochelenko 1986; Leriche 1986a; Leriche and Callot 1986).

On ceramics, Lyonnet 1985 provides a review of the evidence from Afghanistan of all periods; Lyonnet 1998 is a more focussed discussion of the implications of the ceramic evidence for settled-nomadic relations in Bactria-Sogdiana of the last centuries BC; Lyonnet 2010 compares the Hellenistic ceramics from Ai Khanoum and Kok-tepe; and Gardin 1986 takes a wider chronological perspective on movements of pots and movements of people in Bactria. Several other articles by J.-C. Gardin raise methodological and theoretical questions, particularly with regard to the problems posed by pottery being published separately from the other finds from excavations, or at a considerable time-lag (Gardin 1977; Gardin 1985b, with an English translation at <www.arkeotek.org>, accessed 25 October 2010, is a crucial study of the ceramic material from Ai Khanoum and the eastern Bactria survey).

Graeco-Bactrian and Indo-Greek jewellery has been the subject of two short studies: Neva 2008 on Central Asia and Chandra 1979 on the Indo-Greek regions.

5.2 Sites: Bactria, Sogdiana, Margiana, Chorasmia

This section will discuss archaeological sites and field survey areas in the regions to the north of the Hindu Kush: ancient Bactria, Sogdiana and Margiana, with a digression into material from Chorasmia, to the south of the Aral Sea. These names do not conform exactly to any well-defined geographical or political entities, at any period, and a degree of terminological flexibility is desirable. But there are certain modern archaeological naming conventions which it makes sense to outline and to follow here. 'Bactria' refers to the region on either side of the river Oxus/Amu-darya, covering territories in what is now Afghanistan, Tajikistan and Uzbekistan in the Upper Amu-darya Basin. Wherever ancient political frontiers lay at any given period – and that between Bactria and Sogdiana seems sometimes to have been along the Oxus, sometimes further to the north, around the Iron Gates at Derbent (Section 5.2.5) – inter-regional ties were always close, and the material culture of this 'archaeological Bactria' has a certain coherence (see e.g. Rapin 2007, 31; but see also Lyonnet 1993, who emphasises internal variations in material culture within this region). For a longer-term overview of the sites of northern Bactria, see Pugachenkova and Rtveladze 1990. Within Bactria, a division into four sectors is recognised in many publications, whether this is explicitly stated or tacitly followed. These divisions match different riverine catchment areas (and, broadly speaking, modern international borders) along both banks of the Oxus. Sector I is in the north-east, the north bank of the Oxus in what is now Tajikistan. Sites here include Takht-i Sangin. Sector II lies immediately to the south of this, centred around the major sites of Ai Khanoum and Shortughai and their hinterland. Sector III, to the south-west, includes the sites in and around the Bactra oasis, and Sector IV comprises the valley of the Surkhan-darya, which enters the Oxus from the north, and adjacent territory. Gardin 1985b provides the clearest outline of these divisions, with maps; Stride 2007 proposes a similar segmentation of 'Bactria' into regions centred on the irrigable deltas of the Amu-darya's tributary rivers. I will not use Gardin's terminology here, but it may be seen that my section divisions do roughly follow his, and Stride's, schemata.

Sogdiana and Margiana are still less precisely defined. Sogdiana is the region to the north of Bactria, around the valley of the Zeravshan, and had only fairly loose political or cultural ties to it. The position of Samarkand in relation to the Seleucid or Graeco-Bactrian states, as reflected in its material culture, will be discussed below. The 'Iron Gates' at Derbent are the closest we have to an archaeologically-attested frontier between Bactria and Sogdiana. Margiana is to the north-west, in modern Turkmenistan, where the Murghab river flows from the Hindu Kush into the Kara Kum desert. Before disappearing altogether, the Murghab forms an inland delta which supported cities of the Bronze Age Bactria Margiana Archaeological Complex (BMAC). Little material has so far been found in Margiana which is contemporary to the Achaemenid or Hellenistic periods, but it is certainly there to be found (Section 5.2.9). Ancient Chorasmia was centred on the Oxus/Amu-darya delta on the southern shores of the (now-former) Aral Sea.

5.2.1 Takht-i Sangin and the North-East

For an overview of archaeological research in southern Tajikistan (up to the early 1980s) see Litvinskij 1985.

Takht-i Sangin, the 'Temple of the Oxus' and the 'Treasure of the Oxus':

Takht-i Sangin lies near the junction of the Vakhsh (upper Oxus) and Pyandzh rivers. Along with the site of Takht-i Kobad, it was one of two ancient fortresses in the area guarding the right-hand bank of the Oxus. Excavations have revealed continuity of occupation and cult activity at the Temple of the Oxus at Takht-i Sangin from the Achaemenid to the Kushan periods, although the temple building itself appears to be an early Seleucid foundation. Given its size and the unusually heavy use of stone architecture for the region, Seleucid royal patronage is a possibility.

There is, at present, comparatively little evidence on the temple's wider urban context. The site had stone fortifications and contained a sizeable settlement, from which the remains of columns and carved stone architectural elements have been reported. There was a necropolis of the Kushan period, which had been heavily looted. The temple stood inside the stone walls of a fortified citadel, with a surrounding moat. As already noted, the wider region has a much longer settlement history, with a Bronze Age cemetery in the vicinity, and remains of another fort and settlement site just downstream at Takht-i Kobad.

The Oxus Treasure (Dalton 1964), the great hoard of Achaemenid gold now in the British Museum, was found either at Takht-i Sangin or nearby. Debate continues over its precise find-spot. Another, similar hoard, the 'Bactrian Treasure', was acquired more recently by the Miho Museum and is also unprovenanced (catalogue: Miho Museum 2002). Pichikyan regards this as another part of the same treasure (Pichikyan 1997; Pichikyan 1998b; Pichikyan 1998a); Green 2002 views is as a separate cache, Hellenistic in date, from the same geographical region but not necessarily the same find-spot.

The Cyrillic spellings of the names of the two most prolific authors on the Temple of the Oxus, the site's excavators B. A. Litvinskii (Б. А. Литвинский) and I. R. Pichikyan (И. Р. Пичикян), are variously Romanised; I have retained here the transcriptions used in individual publications. In addition to the Russian preliminary and final reports, the site, or rather the temple, has received extensive publication in French, German and English. It is therefore one of the few archaeological sites in the former-Soviet Central Asian Republics of which one can gain a reasonable overview without a knowledge of Russian.

The main reports, in Russian with English summary, are Litvinskii and Pichikyan 2000 (finds, architecture, and religious life at the temple) and Litvinskii 2001 (weaponry). Litvinsky and Pichikyan 2002 is essentially an English translation of the opening part of Litvinskii and Pichikyan 2000. Litvinskiy and Pichikiyan 1981 is a preliminary report in English. The temple and its art have also been the subject of two monograph-length treatments in German: Pitschikjan 1992 and Litvinskij and Pičikjan 2002.

The temple building contained a central room opening on to a courtyard with two wings, each containing a chamber with altars. Two L-shaped corridors passed around and behind the central chamber. Large numbers of votive items were found either stored in the innermost recesses of the corridors, or buried in trenches. Among the finds were large numbers of weapons, and also a few stucco or unfired clay portraits of donors, including diademed figures.

The most commented-upon find was a small altar surmounted by a statuette of a satyr-like figure playing a double pipe, with a Greek inscription by a man with the Iranian name Atrosokes, dedicating to the river Oxus (Litvinskiy and Pichikiyan 1981, 153ff; Litvinskii, et al. 1985). It is to be dated to the second century BC. Bernard 1987 reviews the publication of this ex-voto, and hypothesises the influence of colonists from the Meander valley in Asia Minor on the iconography of the river god of the Oxus. Boyce and Grenet 1991, 173-179, Bernard 1994, and Koch 1993 discuss whether the temple was a 'fire temple' in the Zoroastrian sense, or an image cult with subsidiary fire chambers: the latter appears to be most likely. See also Boyce and Grenet 1991, 179-181 on the deified river Oxus. Drège and Grenet 1987 discuss a Chinese source on a later temple at the site.

Other publications on individual objects or categories of object include: Pichikyan 1987a (altars); Litvinskij and Pičikian 1995b (images of river-deities); Litvinskij and Pičikian 1995a (a handle for a *makhaira* with the image of a griffin); Litvinsky and Pichikjan 1995 (gold plaques); Litvinsky and Pichikian 1998 (an Ionic capital). On the architecture of the sanctuary, and its overall artistic and architectural programme, see Litvinskiy and Pichikyan 1984; Pichikjan 1985; Pichikyan 1987b; Pichikyan 1989; Litvinskii and Pichikian 1994.

More recent excavations are published in Drujinina 2001 (the 1998-1999 field seasons, in German); and also in Druzhinina 2000, Druzhinina 2004, Druzhinina 2005 and Drujinina and Boroffka 2006, which were not available to me.

A project on the small finds from the temple, *Tadjikistan: Votivpraxis im hellenistischen und kuschanzeitlichen Baktrien*, is currently being undertaken by G. Lindström of the Eurasien-Abteilung of the Deutsches Archäologisches Institut (<www.dainst.org>, search query 'Baktrien', accessed 2 November 2010).

Boldai-tepe (Boldajtepe): Boldai-tepe, in the valley of the river Vakhsh upstream from its confluence with the Pyandzh, is another smaller site with layers of third to second centuries BC (Zeimal' 1971; Litvinskii and Zeimal' 1971, 11).

On the archaeology of the Vakhsh Valley in later periods, see Litvinskii and Solokov'ev 1985.

Tamošo Tepe: The core of the site of Tamošo Tepe, in the Yavan valley, a more northerly tributary of the Vakhsh, is said to date to the third – second centuries BC, but I have been unable to locate a copy of the publication on which this report is based (Abdullaev 1979; reported in Litvinskij and Zejmal' 2004, 14).

Kei-Kobad-Shah and the Kafirnigan Valley: Soviet-era archaeological activities in the valley of the Kafirnigan River, parallel to the valley of the Vakhsh to the west, are conveniently summarised in English in Frumkin 1970, 66-70. See also the original Russian publications of D'yakonov 1950, D'yakonov 1953, D'yakonov 1956, Mandel'shtam and Pevzner 1958, and later Sedov 1987, on the Kafirnigan Valley and Kobadian region. Of especial interest is the fortified settlement site at Kei-Kobad-Shah, with layers of the Graeco-Bactrian and Kushan periods. In the regional chronological sequence, Kobadian II represents the third-second centuries BC, and Kobadian III the first century BC – first century AD.

Saksanokhur: The modern Parkhar/Farchor district in south-eastern Tajikistan lies on the Afghan border, and the ancient settlement of Saksanokhur, near the confluence of the Oxus/Amu-darya with the Qizil-su, is thus only around 35 km north-east of Ai Khanoum as the crow flies. The site should therefore be considered alongside Ai Khanoum and its hinterland as much as with other archaeological sites of southern Tajikistan. Saksanokhur was excavated by Soviet teams in 1966-1967 and 1973-1977, and appears to have since been destroyed (Mukhitdinov 1968; Litvinskii and Mukhitdinov 1969; I have been unable to locate published reports of the later seasons). Although the excavators date occupation at the site back to the Graeco-Bactrian period, Bernard 1970, 312-313, suggests that the possible re-use of architectural elements, such as column capitals, from Ai Khanoum may have confused the dating. In addition to a large fortified manor house of the second century BC, comparable in some respects to domestic archtecture at Ai Khanoum (Bernard 1970, 312-313), other, more modest, dwellings and workshops were also excavated.

Kuliab: One of the two new Greek inscriptions published in Bernard, et al. 2004 is said to have come from Kuliab in southern Tajikistan (Chapter 6, Section 6.2.2.1). Nothing appears to be known of any Graeco-Bactrian remains in the vicinity, although the inscription's mention of a 'Grove of Zeus' is tantalising. It should be noted that the modern city (also transcribed 'Kulyob' or 'Kulob') is one of the largest in Tajikistan, and may simply have been where the inscription was acquired.

5.2.2 Ai Khanoum and its Hinterland

City

A summary account of the excavations at Ai Khanoum could easily occupy a book in itself. The purpose of this overview is not to provide a comprehensive account of the city and its remains, but rather a guide to publications and, in particular, to the publication of finds and structures not included in the final series of reports *Fouilles d'Aï Khanoum*.

Ai Khanoum, at the junction of the rivers Oxus/Amu-darya and Kokcha, remains the only extensively-excavated urban site of the Hellenistic period in Bactria. The French archaeologist Jules Barthoux visited the site and wrote a description of it in 1926, although no further investigation was undertaken at that time (Tarzi 1996). It had also been visited by the Scottish explorer Lt. John Wood in 1838 (Bernard and Francfort 1978, 33-38). Modern excavations were undertaken by the DAFA between 1964 and 1978. Bernard 2001 provides a retrospective of the excavations, and a report on the more recent fate of the site, also covered in Besenval, et al. 2002. Articles introducing or summarising the finds from the site include Schlumberger 1965, Frye 1966, Bernard 1967a and P. Bernard 1982 (important articles in English for an educated popular audience), and Rapin 1990.

The internal 'street plan' of Ai Khanoum is known in broad lines. The public buildings, and apparently also the main zone of habitation, lay in the Lower City, the wide plain between the rivers Oxus and Kokcha. The Upper City ('acropolis') was more sparsely occupied, with smaller houses, a stepped podium for some religious purpose, and, at the far south-eastern corner, the fortified citadel. The main street entered the Lower City by the northern gate, and along this street are ranged the theatre, main temple, and the lesser-known buildings to the south (including the 'arsenal'). An extramural temple sits just to one side of the continuation of this road beyond the northern city walls. The city's necropolis was also outside the northern walls, under the slope of the acropolis; one mausoleum has been excavated. A second grouping of public buildings was accessed via the monumental *propylaea* leading off the main street. These include the palace/administrative quarter with its treasury, the shrine of the city's probable founder, Kineas, a second mausoleum with a stone burial vault and the gymnasium. The less-explored area to the south of the latter contained a pool of some sort. This zone beyond the *propylaea* is therefore occupied by institutions with key civic functions or associations. Secondary access routes are less clear. It seems that a road linked the southern residential quarter (dominated by large houses) with the area of the gymnasium, providing a direct connection, a 'back door', which by-passed the *propylaea*.

Liger 1979, a *Maîtrise* thesis which unfortunately remains unpublished, considers the urban layout of the city. Bernard 1981, 111ff, addresses the question of urbanism, and takes the reader on a tour of Ai Khanoum from the point of view of an ancient visitor to the city. Little has been published in the way of aerial views or general survey of the site: see the plates to Leriche 1986b. Surface survey and such aerial photographs reveal something of the general plan of the city beyond the excavated areas, such as the outlines of additional houses in the southern residential quarter, and of a number of mausolea in the extramural necropolis. Some interesting three-dimensional reconstructions of the city have been made for a television documentary (Lecuyot 2005; Lecuyot 2007).

The site's chronology varies from publication to publication, as does the system of numbering of different architectural phases (quite understandable, given the detail of the preliminary reports and the promptness with which they apeared). The discussion of Gardin 1985a on the unpublished ceramic data from Ai Khanoum and its chronological implications should be read with the original reports (English translation at <www.arkeotek.org>, accessed 25 October 2010). Many of the buildings in the city are oriented along the same axis as the main street, roughly NNE-SSW. Most publications adopt the convention of simplifying this to North-South. Fussman's (Fussman 1996) review essay on Ai Khanoum clarifies many such points, and critiques the excavations and their publication. Likewise, Lerner 2003-2004 provides an important critical discussion of the city's early chronology and the various dating criteria (ceramic, palaeographic, architectural) used by the excavators in their subsequent publications.

Given the evidence of earlier occupation in the city's hinterland (see below), and the site's strategic advantages, it seems unlikely that there was not some Achaemenid settlement on the site of the later Hellenistic city (something which is, refreshingly, taken as patent by Lerner 2003-2004). On the evidence for such a settlement, see Bernard and Francfort 1978, 12-14; and on Alexander and Ai Khanoum, Paul Bernard 1982a, a refutation of Bosworth 1981's arguments that Alexander campaigned in eastern Bactria in 328 BC. On local pre-Hellenistic traditions of craftsmanship, from the materials at Ai Khanoum, see Guillaume 1985. The generally-accepted date for the sack and abandonment of the city is c. 145 BC, but a further review of the evidence for this precise date would be welcome (see especially the publications on the fortifications, below, for evidence of attack, and the mass burial in the orchestra of the theatre, which may be the remains of a massacre).

Eight volumes of reports on the site have been published in the series *Fouilles d'Aï Khanoum*, within the umbrella-series of the *Mémoires de la Délégation Archéologique Française en Afghanistan*. Many parts of the site remain unpublished in final form: to give only a few examples, the arsenal, an unidentified public building on the main street, and areas to the north and west of the administrative quarter. For these, the preliminary reports (listed below) must still be consulted.

- *FAKh* I (*MDAFA* XXI), Bernard 1973: Preliminary report on the 1965-1968 field seasons. The administrative quarter, temenos of Kineas, ceramics, statuary, small finds, coins, inscriptions, the geology of the site. 2 Vols.

- *FAKh* II (*MDAFA* XXVI), Guillaume 1983: The propylaea on the main street. Also includes a bibliography of the site –c. 1983.

- *FAKh* III (*MDAFA* XXVII), Francfort 1984: The santuary of the *temple à niches indentées* (*temple à redans*).

- *FAKh* IV (*MDAFA* XXVIII), Bernard 1985: Coins (non-hoard); Graeco-Bactrian history (including: Arachosia and the treaty between Seleucus I and Chandragupta Maurya; the era of Eucratides; coins of Eucratides outside Central Asia; the Branchidae; the mercenary revolt of 323 BC).

- *FAKh* V (*MDAFA* XXIX), Leriche 1986b: The fortifications and associated monuments. Includes both the city walls of the lower city and the fortifications on the acropolis.

- *FAKh* VI (*MDAFA* XXX), Veuve 1987: The gymnasium, including information on the post-Greek occupation.

- *FAKh* VII (*MDAFA* XXXI), Guillaume and Rougeulle 1987: Small finds.

- *FAKh* VIII (*MDAFA* XXXIII), Rapin 1992: The treasury; Graeco-Bactrian history (especially the second century BC and Graeco-Bactrian invasion of India); units of measurement at Ai Khanoum; Graeco-Bactrian chronology; bibliography of Greek inscriptions and literary texts from Central Asia.

The original reports were primarily published in the *Comptes-rendus de l'Académie des inscriptions et belles-lettres*, with some articles also in the *Bulletin de l'École Française d'Extrême Orient* and the *Bulletin de Correspondance Hellénique*. All can be read online via the *Persée* portal (<www.persee.fr>).

- Schlumberger 1965: the discovery of the city, with an overview.

- Schlumberger and Bernard 1965: discovery, preliminary survey, opening of six initial trenches; finds (ceramics, stone vases, terracotta roof tiles and antefixes, architectural fragments).

- Bernard 1966: brief report on the first season of excavations.

- Bernard 1967b: second season of excavations; palace/administrative quarter, herôon of Kineas, column capitals, statue from the gymnasium.

- P. Bernard 1968: third season of excavations; palace/administrative quarter, southern residential quarter, gymnasium.

- Bernard 1969: fourth season of excavations: administrative quarter (this name is now preferred over '*palais*'), house in the southern residential quarter, trench on the acropolis, temple ('*temple à redans*').

- Bernard 1970: 1969 season of excavations; administrative quarter, house in the southern quarter, fortifications of the lower city, *temple à redans* and its sanctuary (including first publication of the Cybele medallion), ceramics.

- Bernard 1971: 1970 season of excavations; administrative quarter, house in the southern quarter, *temple à redans* and its sanctuary, ostrakon in Aramaic script, Greek vase inscriptions (very briefly reported), plaster mouldings, coins (including Indian and Indo-Greek), ceramics.

- Bernard 1972: 1971 season of excavations; extramural necropolis and mausoleum, sanctuary of the temple à redans, administrative quarter, restoration, ceramics, coins, Aramaic-script ostrakon.

- Bernard 1974: 1972 and 1973 excavation seasons; house outside the walls, extramural temple (provisionally '*bâtiment hors-les-murs*'), administrative quarter, sanctuary of the temple à redans, fortifications of the lower city (including a tower), diverse finds.

- Bernard 1975: 1974 season of excavations; administrative quarter (including mosaic), stone-vault mausoleum ('*mausolée au caveau de pierre*'), gymnasium, ceramics, preliminary survey of the city's hinterland (see following section: 'Hinterland').

- Bernard 1976: 1975 season of excavations; palace (formerly the administrative quarter), gymnasium (including sun dials), extramural temple, fortifications of the lower city, fountain by the Oxus, theatre.

- Bernard, et al. 1976: 1974 season of excavations; administrative quarter, stone-vault mausoleum and its burials, gymnasium, ceramics.

- Bernard 1978: 1976 and 1977 seasons of excavations; gymnasium, fountain and fortifications by the Oxus, theatre (including burials in the orchestra), propylaea on the main street, palace (including treasury and Greek texts), south-eastern residential quarter.

- P. Bernard 1980: 1978 season of excavations; propylaea, gymnasium, palace treasury, public building on the main street (adjacent to the temple sanctuary and administrative quarter), arsenal, acropolis (including post-Graeco-Bactrian necropolis).

- Bernard, et al. 1980: 1978 season of excavations; gymnasium, propylaea, palace (treasury and courtyards), public building on the main street, arsenal, fortifications of the upper city and citadel.

Several specialised studies have been devoted to individual elements of the city and categories of finds: on Corinthian capitals see Paul Bernard 1968; and on coins Audouin and Bernard 1973 and Audouin and Bernard 1974 (Indian and Indo-Greek), Bernard and Guillaume 1980, and Holt 1981.

Temples and religious practice: See, in general, the discussion of Downey 1988, 63-76, who provides a comparative treatment of both the city's temples and the podium on the acropolis.

The *temple à niches indentées / temple à redans* and its sanctuary: Downey 1988, 65-73; Grenet 1991 (cult); Mairs forthcoming-b ('Mesopotamian' elements, and the temple's position within the city).

The extramural temple: Downey 1988, 73-75.

The podium on the acropolis: Downey 1988, 75-76; Boyce and Grenet 1991, 181-184 (drawing on unpublished material); for potential regional comparandanda, see Sections 5.2.4: Sites of the Sherabad-darya, on Pashmak-tepe and 5.2.4: Sites of the Surkhan-darya and its Watershed, on Pshak-tepe, as well as the discussion of Shenkar 2007 on such podiums in Achaemenid religious architecture.

Gymnasium: Veuve 1982 and Savoie 2007 (the sundials).

Treasury: Rapin 1987; Rapin 1996a (an English translation of parts of Rapin 1992, on Indian art). See Chapter 6, Section 6.2.3.1 on the economic texts from the treasury, and Chapter 6, Section 6.2.4.1 on the literary texts.

Fortifications: Leriche 1974; Leriche and Thoraval 1979 (the fountain by the Oxus wall); Leriche and Callot 1986 (comparisons with Dura Europos).

Hinterland

Ai Khanoum was placed in some much-needed geographical and chronological context by the implementation, from 1974 to 1978, of a field survey project in eastern Bactria, with its focus on the immediate agricultural hinterland of the city (the 'plaine d'Ai Khanoum' or 'plaine de Dasht-i Qala'). The results of this survey revealed much about the nature and extent of long-term settlement and irrigation in the region – such as its dense Bronze Age occupation – and the economic and agricultural foundations upon which Ai Khanoum was built. Satellite photographs of the plain today reveal intensive modern agricultural exploitation and settlement (to view on Google Maps, enter the co-ordinates 37°10'24"N 69°24'49"E).

The results of this survey programme are published in the three volumes of *Prospections archéologiques en Bactriane orientale (1974-1978)* (Gentelle 1989: palaeogeographical data; Lyonnet 1997: ceramics and chronology; Gardin 1998: sites and settlement patterns), with preliminary reports on the project, its objectives and methodology, in Gardin and Gentelle 1976, Gentelle 1978, Gardin and Gentelle 1979, Gardin and Lyonnet 1979, and Gardin 1980. On the historical geography of the region of Ai Khanoum see Bernard and Francfort 1978. The survey team sought to map irrigation networks and to identify sites by following the lines of the still-visible ancient irrigation channels, a methodology which brought fruitful results ('sites' are broadly defined, the term merely indicating concentrations of archaeological material such as pot-sherds, and not necessarily the remains of habitation). The presence and size of canals were themselves used to deduce further information on expanse of land cultivated and the population levels which might be supported. The methodologies employed, their theoretical basis and practical application are amply and transparently documented in the publications. Data from the eastern Bactria survey was to be encorporated into an archaeological GIS of Afghanistan announced in Padwa 2004 (see above).

The settlement history of the region is, as demonstrated by the survey, of considerable chronological depth, and its connections with regions beyond north-eastern Bactria longstanding. The site of Shortughai, discovered by the survey team in 1975, appears to have been a commercial outpost of the Indus Civilisation (Francfort 1989). Connections with the Indus Civilisation may be documented in the material culture of the region throughout the Chalcolithic and Bronze Ages (Lyonnet 1977; Lyonnet 1981; Francfort 1985; Jarrige 1985). On the Bronze Age irrigation of eastern Bactria, see Gardin 1984, with a useful summary of practical and methodological issues in English, and on pre-Hellenistic sites, including fortifications, Gardin 1981 and Gardin 1995. The major fortified site in the vicinity of Ai Khanoum before the Macedonian conquest was some 3 km to the north at Kohna Qala (the 'Ville ronde'), a citadel on the left bank of the Oxus with two concentric surrounding walls (visible on satallite photographs). Its earliest occupation dates to the Iron Age. Evidence for such Iron Age or Achaemenid settlement occurs across the survey area as a whole. The survey teams found that river courses and climatic conditions did not appear to have altered appreciably over the periods investigated, and that canals tended to follow the lines of earlier irrigation channels as a matter of course. Although such important long-term continuities may be traced, however, the plain of Ai Khanoum does appear to have experienced an intensification in irrigation works and increase in population corresponding to the period of the Greek settlement.

Among the advantages and attractions of the site of Ai Khanoum – and of earlier settlements in its vicinity – are: control over routes of trade, invasion and pastoral transhumance, both north and south of the Oxus, by river and on land; more specifically, control of the routes down from the mountains of Badakshan, the only exploited source of lapis lazuli in the ancient world, and of other precious metals and minerals; the agricultural potential, with irrigation, of the flat land between the rivers and the hills; and various natural protuberances which might readily be fortified, such as the Ai Khanoum 'citadel' and 'acropolis'. Lapis lazuli occurs from a very early period in regions far distant from Bactria (see e.g. Bavay 1997 on lapis in Predynastic Egypt) and appears to be a key reason for the establishment of the Indus Civilisation outpost at Shortughai. But it is difficult to find much information on lapis extraction, working and trade in eastern Bactria itself (see Bernard and Francfort 1978, 49-51). The presence of unworked blocks of lapis in the Treasury at Ai Khanoum is noted briefly in Bernard and Francfort 1978, 9. To my knowledge, no archaeological work has been carried out at the mines. On the ecological conditions under which irrigation in eastern Bactria was developed see Gentelle 1985 and Trichet and Ruben 1985.

The archaeological survey of eastern Bactria appears as a case study, and is 'reviewed' favourably, in several multi-regional explorations of field survey results and methodology (Banning 1996, 28-29; Hellenistic: Alcock 1994, 186-187; Alcock 1993), as well as in Francfort and Lecomte's study of irrigation in Central Asia up to the Achaemenid period (Francfort and Lecomte 2002, 637-640), and Lyonnet's brief article on the transition from Achaemenid to Seleucid control in Bactria and in Syria (Lyonnet 1994).

The site of *Saksanokhur* (Section 5.2.1), lies only around 35 km north-east of Ai Khanoum on the north bank of the Oxus.

5.2.3 Bactra and its Oasis

Bactra (Zariaspa): Bactra, modern Balkh, was the capital of the Achaemenid satrapy of Bactria and of the Graeco-Bactrian kingdom. Polybios (*Histories* 11.34) records that the city, then controlled by the Graeco-Bactrian king Euthydemos, was besieged by Antiochos III on his eastern anabasis. Despite its relative historical prominence (Ai Khanoum, in contrast, is not mentioned for certain in any ancient historical works, and even the question of its ancient name remains to be settled), the archaeological history of Bactra has largely been one of frustration. The site's great antiquity and vast size make it a formidable challenge to excavators, and those who have approached the site in search of material of a specific period (most often Hellenistic) have tended to come away disappointed.

Bactra was a priority for the newly-established DAFA in the 1920s, and Alfred Foucher spent a gruelling and largely unrewarding eighteen-month field season there in 1923-1925, recounted in Foucher and Bazin-Foucher 1942/47, Vol. I, 55-121. Bernard 2007 provides a detailed discussion of Foucher's work at Bactra, its intellectual and political context, and the various practical and methodological factors which limited the success of these excavations. It was Foucher's experience at Bactra which led him to coin the now-notorious term 'Bactrian mirage'. The DAFA returned to conduct two field seasons in 1947 (Schlumberger 1949; Gardin 1957). Work in the mid-1950s focussed on the city's fortifications (1953: Young 1955; 1955 and 1956: Le Berre and Schlumberger 1964).

Before official excavations were recommenced at Bactra by the DAFA in the early 2000s, the discovery of architectural elements such as Corinthian and Ionian stone column capitals by less-official excavators at the site of Tepe Zargaran finally confirmed the existence of a 'Greek city' of Bactra (Besenval, Bernard and Jarrige 2002, 1403-1411). Several field seasons have since been undertaken, with promising results and the discovery of material dating not just to the Graeco-Bactrian period, but to the preceding Achaemenid levels of the city (Bernard, et al. 2007; Besenval and Marquis 2007; Besenval and Marquis 2008).

A presentation of the excavations may be found on the *France Diplomatie* website, accessed 8 October 2010 (<http://www.diplomatie.gouv.fr/fr/actions-france_830/archeologie_1058/les-carnets-archeologie_5064/asie-oceanie_5069/afghanistan-bactres_14847/index.html>). Brief reports and updates may also be found on the DAFA website (<www.dafa.af>).

Cheshme Shafa (*Cheshma Shafa*): The most recent DAFA team to work at Bactra have also undertaken survey of the city's hinterland and several seasons of excavations at the site of Cheshme Shafa, a fortified pass to the south of Bactra where the Balkh-ab river descends onto the plain (Besenval and Marquis 2007; Besenval and Marquis 2008). The excavation of Achaemenid and Kushan levels at the site provides another important opportunity to examine the longer-term settlement history of the region, of which the Graeco-Bactrian period was only a part. For updates on research at Cheshme Shafa, see the web resources cited for Bactra, above.

Dil'berdzhin (Дильберджин, also transcribed *Delbarjin, Dilberjin, Dil'berdjin, Dil'berdžin, Dilberdzhin*; but not to be confused with Dal'verzin-tepe in Uzbekistan, Section 5.2.4: Sites of the Surkhan-darya and its Watershed): The ancient town of Dil'berdzhin lies in the northern part of the Bactra oasis, around 40km north-west of Bactra itself, and was excavated by a joint Soviet-Afghan expedition from 1969-1973 (site reports: Kruglikova 1974; Kruglikova and Pugachenkova 1977; Kruglikova 1986; further articles: Vainberg and Kruglikova 1976; Dolgorukov 1984; Pugachenkova 1984; in French: Kruglikova 1977). Like nearby Zhiga-tepe (see below), the site's chronology has been disputed (Fitzsimmons 1994; Fitzsimmons 1996; Lo Muzio 1999): the analyses of the original reports should be read critically and with caution.

The majority of the finds and architectural remains from Dil'berdzhin date to the Kushan period or later and thus fall outside the scope of this survey. The attribution of the early phases of the town itself, and moreover of the 'Temple of the Dioscuri' to the Graeco-Bactrian period may be little more than wishful thinking, but the Greek religious iconography in the frescos from this temple, and the question of the cult of Greek deities in Kushan Bactria, deserves to be considered here briefly. Among religious figures and motifs of diverse cultural origins, the temple contained a fresco of the Dioscuri with an iconography which is recognisably Greek (Kruglikova 1976a; Lo Muzio 1999). On the 'Athena' of Dil'berdzhin see Grenet 1987a.

Zhiga-tepe: The site of Zhiga-tepe, 5km east of Dil'berdzhin in the Bactra oasis, was excavated by a Soviet-Afghan team in 1974 and 1976 (Pugachenkova 1979, with abstract in French; Pidaev 1984). On the Zhiga-tepe's disputed chronology, see Fitzsimmons 1994 and Fitzsimmons 1996. The site, a raised tell surrounded by a double enclosure wall, may have been a cult place of some sort (there are parallels with Bronze Age Bactrian religious sites such as Dashly-III: Sarianidi 1984). It also yielded the Greek metric dedication or – more probably, given its apparent reference to Hades – funerary inscription, on a ceramic plaque, of a man named Diogenes (Canali De Rossi 2004 No. 304; Kruglikova 1977, 425, fig. 16; Pugachenkova 1979, 74–75; Vinogradov in Litvinskii, Vinogradov and Pichikyan 1985, 104–105; Bernard 1987, 112–113; also noted in Chapter 6, Section 6.2.2.1, below). Nothing further is known of the inscription's archaeological context, or of any cemetery of which it may have formed a part.

Emshi-tepe: Emshi-tepe is a large fortified urban site around 4 km north-east of the town of Shibarghan, south-west of Dil'berdzhin. It was the subject of a very brief description in Barger 1941, 45. The Afghan-Soviet excavations from 1969 onwards are published in Kruglikova and Mustamandi 1970, Kruglikova and Sarianidi 1971, Kruglikova 1973 and with a summary by Kruglikova and Sarianidi in Kruglikova 1976b, 3-20 (I have not had access to the first two items listed). Francfort 1979, 23-26, gives an overview of site and discusses the Hellenistic fortifications. On potsherds with Greek letters from Emshi-tepe, see Chapter 6, Section 6.2.3.1.

5.2.4 Termez, the Surkhan-darya and the North-West

This section begins with the two major sites on this section of the Oxus/Amu-darya with Graeco-Bactrian levels (Termez and Kampyr-tepe), then lists two clusters of sites from south to north along the valleys of two tributaries of the Amu-darya: the Surkhan-darya (upstream of Termez) and the Sherabad-darya, which leads towards the Iron Gates at Derbent. Due to its use for irrigation, the waters of the Sherabad-darya now no longer reach the Amu-darya. Leriche, Pidaev, Gelin, Abdoullaev and Fourniau 2001 (available online through Google Books) contains a useful map of the region.

Termez: Termez, controlling a strategic position on the north bank of the Oxus at its junction with the Surkhan-darya, is another extensive, multi-period site (see Leriche 2001b; Leriche and Pidaev 2007 and in general the articles in Leriche, Pidaev, Gelin, Abdoullaev and Fourniau 2001, available online at Google Books). It was part of an extended network of fortresses controlling strategic points on the routes north of the Oxus. Leriche and Pidaev 2008 provide a well-illustrated introduction to and overview of the site, with an account of the history of the excavations, intended to be accessible to the general reader with no Russian (pp. 25-40 cover the Hellenistic period). Material of the Hellenistic period is for the most part buried under the levels of the Kushan period, when the settlement expanded and grew in importance, but it is still possible to gain a sense of the site's layout under the Graeco-Bactrians. On Alexander the Great, the Seleucids and the Graeco-Bactrian period at Termez, see Leriche 2002 and Pidaev 2003. Three sites in the same vicinity, Shor-tepe, Termez and Kampyr-tepe (see below) appear to have achieved prominence under the Achaemenids, Graeco-Bactrians and Kushans respectively, declining in importance or disappearing altogether in other periods. In the Hellenistic period, Termez was nevertheless the site of a citadel-fortress on the bank of the Oxus, a zone of habitation outside the walls of this fortress, and to the north a temple and cult platform, still (as of Leriche and Pidaev 2008) in course of excavation. It is possible that the cult platform was an open-air altar of the sort found at several other Bactrian sites, including Ai Khanoum.

The *Bactriane du Nord* website (<http://jeanbaptiste.houal.free.fr/index.htm>, accessed 16 October 2010) provides information on excavations at Termez, and other activities of the MAFOuz de Bactriane. This website also contains information on work at Khaytabad-tepe, upstream from Termez along the Surkhan-darya, which may also have levels of the Graeco-Bactrian period and certainly has levels of the Achaemenid period (Leriche and Annaev 1996, 295-298). A 3D reconstruction of the Kushan period fortifications at Termez (Tchingiz-tepe), by J.-B. Houal, may also be viewed online (<http://www.archeo.ens.fr/spip.php?article1041>, accessed 16 October 2010). For later periods at Termez, including the Buddhist monastery at Kara-tepe, the reader is referred in the first instance to Leriche and Pidaev 2008 and the papers in Leriche, Pidaev, Gelin, Abdoullaev and Fourniau 2001, where further bibliography may be followed up.

Kampyr-tepe (Kampir-tepe): Kampyr-tepe was a fortified settlement guarding a crossing point on the Oxus, 30 km west of its confluence with the Surkhan darya at Termez. Its active life lasted from around the third century BC to the second century AD: its decline coincides with the growth of Termez, and Kampyr-tepe itself had usurped the position of the nearby Achaemenid site of Shor-tepe (Pugachenkova 1987; discussed briefly in Leriche 2007, 132-133). The excavations are published in the series *Материалы Тохаристанской экспедиции. Археологические исследования Кампыртепа* (*Materials from the Tokharistan Expedition: Archaeological Research at Kampyr-tepe*, Tashkent: Rtveladze 2000; Rtveladze 2001; Rtveladze 2002; Rtveladze 2006; Rtveladze 1984b is an earlier report). Rtweladse 2009 provides a well-illustrated account in German. The Kampyr-tepe website, in Russian, contains plans and photographs of the site (<http://www.kampyrtepa.narod.ru/>, accessed 9 October 2010). The online archives of *San'at* magazine have some relevant articles, in English and Russian (<http://www.sanat.orexca.com/>, accessed 9 October 2010). Rtveladze 1999 provides a brief, popular account in French, and a somewhat effusive BBC report of 2004 bills the site as 'Uzbekistan's Best Kept Secret' (Whitlock 18 April 2004). On the citadel and fortifications see Rusanov 1994, Savchuk 1989 and Azimov 2001; on the numismatic data (mostly Kushan and Parthian), Rtveladze 1994; and on arms and depictions of arms from the site Nikonorov and Savchuk 1992 and Rtveladze 1995. The majority of the material so far published is of the Kushan period, although Graeco-Bactrian material is certainly present, and stratigraphic studies have established the periodisation of the site. There are three broken fragments of ceramic vessels with Greek economic writings of the same nature as those excavated at Ai Khanoum, as well as several small scraps of papyrus with Greek letters, about which little or no further information appears to have been published (Rtveladze 1995; see 5.2.2, above, on Ai Khanoum and Chapter 6, 6.2.3.1 on the Kampyr-tepe texts and comparative material from other sites).

The Surkhan-darya – Survey and GIS: The valley of the Surkhan-darya river, which flows into the Oxus/Amu-darya from the north, contains a number of sites with Graeco-Bactrian and Kushan remains, the most important of which are listed in the following paragraphs. Leriche 2001a provides a bibliography by site and period. On the region in the Bronze and Iron Ages, see Rtveladze and Sagdullaev 1985. I will not make reference to individual Bronze Age sites in what follows, unless they also contain strata from later periods, nor to later sites with no definite evidence of occupation in the Graeco-Bactrian period. See also Rtveladze 1990 on the historical geography and archaeological sites of the Surkhan-darya valley, and the location of the Iron Gates.

The Surkhan-darya valley has been subject to extensive surface survey, as well as investigation using modern technology such as satellite imagery, geomagnetic survey and Google Earth (Stančo 2009), by various Soviet, Uzbek and international missions. The research questions, methodology and results of these surveys are summarised most accessibly in Stride 2007, with especial emphasis on the potential for human exploitation of the region's landscapes and the historical importance of transhumant pastoralism. As with Termez (see above), the reader is referred to the edited volume of Leriche, Pidaev, Gelin, Abdoullaev and Fourniau 2001, which contains articles on the history of earlier research in the region (Pougatchenkova 2001b) and on the more recent work of the MAFOuz de Bactriane (Grenet and Isamiddinov 2001). On survey archaeology and the use of satellite imagery see the chapters of Gentelle 2001, Stride 2001 and Huff, et al. 2001.

The creation of an archaeological GIS for the Surkhan darya region, from diverse data-sources, is outlined in Stride 2004. The potential of Soviet-era ethnographic and environmental studies to contribute to such a database is of especial interest (see also Stride 2007, 103-105). The recent work of the International Pluridisciplinary

Archaeological Expedition in Bactria (IPAEB), including regional studies as well as excavations at sites such as Kara-tepe and Chingiz-tepe, may be consulted in the Expedition's preliminary reports (Gurt, et al. 2007; Gurt, et al. 2008a; Gurt, et al. 2008b; online at the Digital Repository of the Universitat de Barcelona: <http://diposit.ub.edu/dspace/>).

Similar survey projects in the Middle Zeravshan Valley, around Samarkand, will be discussed in Section 5.2.6: Survey Projects.

Sites of the Surkhan-darya and its watershed:

Pshak-tepe: See below, on Pashmak-tepe, and also on this site near the confluence of the Surkhan-darya with the Amu-darya, Askarov 1982 and Duke 1974 (which I have not seen).

Zar-tepe: Zar-tepe was a fortified Kushan town 26 km north-west of Termez, at which coins and ceramics of the Graeco-Bactrian period have also been found.

Khaytabad-tepe: see above on Termez.

Dal'verzin-tepe: Dal'verzin-tepe, some 120 km north-east of Termez in the Surkhan-darya valley, is a major Kushan-period site from which some earlier has also been recovered. Tourgounov 2001 presents a summary of recent excavations, dating the first substantial foundation at the site to between the end of the second century and beginning of the first century BC. It should be noted that, in this region, these dates are post-Graeco-Bactrian.

Evidence nevertheless indicates the pre-existence of a relatively small Graeco-Bactrian period fortification, of the third-second centuries BC, which underwent major expansion and renovations under the Kushans (Tourgounov 1986). The ceramics from these earlier levels present analogies with those of Ai Khanoum, and there are also some Graeco-Bactrian coins from the site. There is no evidence of Achaemenid presence or major Bronze Age settlement at Dal'verzin-tepe, indicating that it is largely a foundation of the Graeco-Bactrian period.

On the Kushan settlement, see, in general, Al'baum 1969, Pugachenkova and Rtveladze 1978 Pougatchenkova 1978 and Paul Bernard 1980. Japanese-Uzbek excavations in the 1990s uncovered further material of the Kushan period and later (Tanabe, et al. 1996). Grenet 1984 (K17) discusses a mausoleum from the site, dated to the end of the Graeco-Bactrian period or period of the nomadic invasions. See Silvi Antonini 1995 and Turgunov 1992 on the later Buddhist temple.

Khalchayan (Khaltchayan): Khalchayan is yet another site with some evidence of Graeco-Bactrian occupation (Pugachenkova 1966, 127) but which, in its excavated form, is essentially Kushan. In the first century BC it became the site of a Yuezhi/Kushan palace, with a set of remarkable clay sculptures which formed part of a dynastic cult. The original excavation reports and accounts of the sculptures may be found in Pugachenkova 1966 and Pugachenkova 1971, with a French summary in Pugachenkova 1965 and more recent discussion of the sculptures and their local Bactrian antecedents in Nehru 1999/2000.

Sites of the Sherabad-darya (Shirabad-darya):

Jandavlattepa (Djandavlattepa; Džandaulattepe): Occupation at Jandavlattepa, in Sherabad district, dates back as far as the Bronze Age. Graeco-Bactrian and Achaemenid levels below the more substantial remains of the Kushan and Sasanian periods yielded some Graeco-Bactrian coins and ceramics typical of northern and eastern Bactria in the Hellenistic period, but, to my knowledge, no architectural structures. On German-Uzbek and later Czech-Uzbek activities at the site, see Huff, Pidaev and Chaydoullaev 2001, 219-221; Abdullaev and Stančo 2003; Abdullaev 2004; Abdullaev and Stančo 2004; Abdullaev and Stančo 2005; Stančo and al. 2005; and Abdullaev and Stančo 2007. The Sherabad region has been subject to a very effective experimental survey using Google Earth (Stančo 2009).

Pashmak-tepe (Pachmak-tepe, Pacmak-tepe): The principal interest of Pashmak-tepe for archaeologists of the Hellenistic period is the comparative material it offers for religious practice at Ai Khanoum. The site lies between the Surkhan-darya and Sherabad-darya. An open-air, stepped altar around 2.6 m in height and 21 m square, constructed of rammed earth, dates to the Achaemenid period. It is very similar in form and dimensions to the open-air altar on the acropolis at Ai Khanoum (Section 5.2.2), and thus provides a valuable local Achaemenid antecedent, allowing us to place Ai Khanoum in a local religious and architectural context. The Pashmak-tepe podium is briefly reported in Pidaev 1974, with fuller details on the site and its environs in Sagdullaev and Khakimov 1976 and Abdullaev 1994 (which I have not been able to consult). Its religious affiliations and similarities to the Ai Khanoum podium are discussed by Boyce and Grenet 1991, 182-183.

Shenkar 2007, 177, discusses the altar from Pashmak-tepe alongside similar, contemporary or near-contemporary, raised terraces for open-air worship at Pshak-tepe in Bactria and Kok-tepe in Sogdiana (Section 5.2.6), and sets them in their wider Iranian context.

5.2.5 Derbent – The 'Iron Gates'

The 'Iron Gates' at Derbent, in the valley of the Sherabaddarya, mark an ancient frontier – but not the only ancient frontier – between Bactria and Sogdiana, and also the effective archaeological boundary between the projects of the Franco-Uzbek missions the *MAFOuz de Sogdiane* and the MAFOuz de Bactriane (see Chapter 5, 5.1.1 on archaeological work in Central Asia in the 1990s and 2000s). Rapin 2007 discusses the MAFOuz excavations at Samarkand, Kok-tepe (Section 5.2.6) and the Iron Gates, and interrelations between them.

The 'Iron Gates' occupy a natural place of defence on the mountainous road between Termez and Samarkand, near the modern village of Derbent. The ancient defensive system consisted of ditches and a massive wall. The first phases of construction of this wall date to the Graeco-Bactrian period. Lyonnet 1998, 153-154, provides a brief discussion of the ceramics, on the basis of which a construction date as early as the reign of Antiochos I is not to be ruled out; she also discusses the relation of the fortifications to the two periods of occupation at Samarkand. On questions of historical geography relevant to the Iron Gates and the various routes which passed through them, see Rtveladze 1990, Grenet and Rapin 1998a, Rapin 1998 and Rapin 2005. Lyonnet 1993 explores the problem of the ancient frontier between Bactria and Sogdiana, with an emphasis on local, intra-regional variations in material culture: but note that this article pre-dates the most recent archaeological activities at Derbent.

Much of the more recent bibliography on the excavations at Derbent is difficult to collate. I have been unable to locate copies of any of the most up-to-date Russian or Central Asian publications in the libraries to which I have access, and even some of the French periodicals in which reports have been published are more than usually obscure (e.g. C. Rapin 2003). A provisional bibliography, compiled in 2007, is available online (<http://www.archeo.ens.fr/IMG/pdf/1BiblioDerbent1.pdf>, accessed 26 October 2010). In the meantime, the reader is well served by Rapin and Rakhmanov 1999's popular article, Rapin's (2007) piece on the activities of the MAFOuz at the Iron Gates and other Sogdian sites, and the survey and critical discussion by Rapin, et al. 2006 (<http://www.archeo.ens.fr/IMG/pdf/3GeogrPF-IMKU35.pdf>, accessed online 4 October 2010).

5.2.6 Maracanda – Samarkand – Afrasiab

Samarkand is one of several large, multiperiod sites in Central Asia which remained occupied until their destruction by the Mongols in AD 1220, and thus present particular challeges to archaeologists interested in their earlier strata (cf. Section 5.2.3 on Bactra and 5.2.9 on Merv). It has most recently been excavated by the MAFOuz de Sogdiane (see also above on the Iron Gates and below on Kok-tepe), updates on the work of which are published in the newsletter *La Timuride*, published by the *Association pour l'Art et l'Histoire Timurides*

(<www.timurides.org/>, accessed 1 November 2010). A brief illustrated summary (- 2007) of these excavations is available online at <http://frantz.grenet.free.fr/index.php?choix=afrasiab> (accessed 1 November 2010). Grenet 2004 discusses the archaeological evidence and written sources on the pre-Mongol city, and gives an especially useful account of the history of archaeological investigation and historical research at the site; for which see also Bernard, et al. 1990. Shishkina 1994 gives an introductory overview in English, with references to several Russian works I have been unable to locate. I have unfortunately not been able to access copies of the reports in the series *Афрасиаб* (*Afrasiab*), published in Tashkent. Samarkand presents the kind of opportunity to combine written and archaeological sources which we lack at sites such as Ai Khanoum (Bernard 1996). Grenet and Rapin 1998b cover the history of of Samarkand through into the Islamic period and provide relevant bibliography.

Many of the studies I cite here note the evidence for a two-phase Greek occupation at Samarkand, the first commencing under Alexander, the second representing a reconquest or reoccupation under Eukratides of Bactria in the first half of the second centry BC. The ceramic evidence, in particular, indicates a hiatus between these phases, IIA and IIB in the reports, and nomadic burials in the vicinity may indicate different settlement patterns by different groups at this period (see e.g. Lyonnet 1998, 152; in general on ceramics from the site: Shishkina 1972 and Lyonnet 1998, 143-151). On the city's fortifications see the articles of Rapin and Isamiddinov 1994 and Chichkina 1986. Samarkand's already considerable defences underwent massive renovation and reconstruction in the Hellenistic period: Greek letters were used as brick-marks in the construction of these (see Chapter 6, Section 6.2.3.1: Samarkand). I have been unable to locate a copy of Inevatkina 2002 on the acropolis fortifications in the mid-first millennium BC. A large public building and grain storage facility of the Hellenistic period have been excavated (Grenet and Isamiddinov 2001, 239-241; Baratin 2010), as well as craft production areas, but the residential areas of the Hellenistic period have proven difficult to locate (Bernard, et al. 1992, 292-294; Bernard, et al. 1996).

Survey projects: On archaeological survey in the Middle Zeravshan Valley, along the same principles – and involving some of the same principals – as the Surkhandarya projects, see Stride, et al. 2009 and Rondelli and Mantellini 2004. Gentelle and Le Tourneau 2007 [2000] report on the use of remote-sensing in the region around Samarkand.

Kok-tepe: Like Samarkand, Kok-tepe, an established Bronze-Iron Age fortified settlement in the middle Zeravshan Valley, appears to have been abandoned only a few decades after the Macedonian conquest (Grenet and Isamiddinov 2001, 237). At Kok-tepe, however, there is no trace of any subsequent major Graeco-Bactrian occupation; burials of nomadic steppe peoples predominate among the post-Hellenistic remains (Rapin

2007; Rapin, et al. 2001). On the Hellenistic material from the site, see most recently Isamiddinov 2010 and Lyonnet 2010 (which were unfortunately not available to me).

Kok-tepe is another site with an Achaemenid-period cult platform, a possible regional precedent for the similar open-air altar at Ai Khanoum (see the bibliography in Section 5.2.3.4: Sites of the Sherabad-darya, on Pashmak-tepe).

5.2.7 Alexandria Eschate – Khujand

Alexandria Eschate: The site of Alexandria 'The Furthest' has been identified as modern Khujand (formerly Leninabad) in Tajikistan, at the entrance to the Ferghana Valley. Despite earlier, Achaemenid, presence in the vicinity, Alexander's decision to found a new fortified city on the Jaxartes/Syr-darya appears to have contributed to a fierce local revolt (Holt 1988, 52-69).

Excavations at the then-Leninabad have revealed evidence of similarities in material culture with other urban sites of the Hellenistic Far East, such as the use of mud bricks marked with Greek letters (as at Samarkand), and some ceramics with forms analogous to those of Ai Khanoum. Soviet excavations of the 1980s are reported in Beljaeva 1986 and N. N. Negmatov 1986. I have not been able to locate these publications, but their contents are summarised by Bernard in *Abstracta Iranica* 10, 1987, No. 176 and No. 203. Numan N. Negmatov 1986 discusses the site and its problems in English. I have also been unable to locate a copy of Hasanov 1998, on the discovery of a strigil and other 'Greek' finds at the nearby site of Nur-tepe (cited by Grenet 2004, 1057, n. 38).

5.2.8 Herat and Areia

Little or nothing known of Achaemenid and Hellenistic – or, indeed, Kushan – city of Herat. By far the most extensive remains are of the Timurid period; in the wider region, some sites of the latter part of the first millennium BC and first part of the first millennium AD have been identified, but have yet to be excavated. Archaeological field survey, excavations and museum work are ongoing as part of the *Herat – Areia Antiqua* project of the Deutsches Archäologisches Institut, Eurasien-Abteilung, directed by U. Franke (<http://www.dainst.org/>, search query 'Herat Afghanistan', accessed 2 November 2010) and the *DAFA* (<http://www.dafa.org.af/index.php?page=fr_Herat>, accessed 2 November 2010). As yet, Franke notes, there is no trace of Alexander at Herat.

Lézire 1964 is an older account of Herat and its history; Rapin 2005 discusses the historical geography of the route between Herat and Begram.

5.2.9 Merv and Margiana

Merv (Antiocheia in Margiana): The present remains of the city of Merv are composed of several continguous settlements of various periods, from the Bronze Age through to its virtual destruction by the Mongols in AD 1221. Excavations have thus far concentrated almost exclusively on material of the Sasanian or Islamic periods, but Hellenistic material is there to be found. See Usmanova 1992 for an overview of the archaeological state-of-affairs in 1992, and the subsequent reports of the International Merv Project (Herrmann, et al. 1993; Herrmann, et al. 1994; Herrmann and Kurbansakhatov 1995; Herrmann, et al. 1996; Herrmann, et al. 1997; Herrmann, et al. 1998; Herrmann, et al. 1999; Herrmann, et al. 2000; Herrmann, et al. 2001; Williams, et al. 2002; Williams, et al. 2003; see also the Ancient Merv Project website at <http://www.ucl.ac.uk/merv/>, accessed 5 October 2010). At Merv, Gyaur-kala is the Hellenistic, or Hellenistic-contemporary, city, Antiocheia in Margiana. Its citadel, Erk-kala, represents the city of the Achaemenid period. On the fortifications of Gyaur-kala see Zavyalov 2007.

The Merv Oasis and Margiana: Unlike the city of Merv, where we know little about the Hellenistic city simply because the levels of the Hellenistic period remain mostly unexcavated, the lack of Hellenistic period material from the wider Merv Oasis poses some serious interpretative problems. The 'Wall of Antiochos' (Strabo IX 10.2) cannot be identified for certain because of the difficulties in dating mud brick constructions. Bader, et al. 1998 argue that is is represented by a pre-Islamic wall relatively close in to the oasis, and not by any of the fortifications further from the city. The evidence of field survey and satellite imagery appears to support the theory that there was a general constriction in the area of settled and irrigated land around the oasis in the Hellenistic period. But this stands in contrast to a picture from historical sources in which the urban settlements and agricultural wealth of the region are stressed (Callieri 1996). Given the problems in dating archaeological remains, and, indeed, artefacts and ceramics, from the region, it must be accepted that much about the extent and nature of the occupation of Margiana in the Hellenistic period remains to be determined. See Koshelenko, et al. 1996 on changing settlement patterns in the Merv Oasis over the longue durée, Salvatori 2008 for a regional picture, and Lecomte 2007 on recent archaeological research in southern Turkmenistan, 2001-2006.

Pilipko 2001 discusses Achaemenid and Hellenistic sites in the neighbouring area he refers to as 'north-western Bactria', along the Oxus/Amu-darya within the borders of modern Turkmenistan.

5.2.10 Chorasmia

Chorasmia (Khwarezm): Chorasmia and its archaeological sites lie outside the scope of this handbook, since the region was beyond the limits of Alexander's campaigns and was at no point part of the Graeco-Bactrian kingdom (see, in general, Helms 1998). It had been an Achaemenid satrapy, but disappears from Persian records and probably ceased to pay tribute in around the mid-fifth century BC (Helms in Khozhaniyazov 2006, 7-8).

Important sites with levels contemporary to the Hellenistic period include Koi-Krylgan-kala (Tolstov and Vainberg 1967) and the sites of the Tash-k'irman oasis, which were abandoned after around the second century AD (Helms, et al. 2001; Helms, et al. 2002; Tash-k'irman Tepe: Betts and Yagodin 2007; and Kazakl'i-yatkan: Helms and Yagodin 1997). Further information on the Tash-k'irman oasis excavations is available on the website of the Karakalpak-Australian Expedition (<http://sydney.edu.au/arts/uscap/uzbekistan/index.shtml>, accessed 9 October 2010). Khozhaniyazov 2006 discusses the region's military architecture form the sixth century BC to the fourth century AD.

For further information on the region's archaeological sites, the *Karakalpak* website provides detailed, illustrated accounts, with maps and Google Earth co-ordinates (<http://www.karakalpak.com/tourancient.html>, accessed 9 October 2010).

5.3 South of the Hindu Kush: The Kabul Region, Arachosia and India

5.3.1 Begram

I provide here only a very brief bibliography on the site of Begram (Alexandria in the Caucasus), restricting myself to excavation reports and some works on Begram's connections with the Greek and Roman world. Almost all of the excavated material comes from the Kushan-period city, although Begram had earlier been the site of a foundation by Alexander. Hackin 1939, Hackin 1954 and Ghirshman 1946 are the fundamental excavation reports. Hackin 1954 contains an initial discussion on Begram's connections with the Graeco-Roman world (Kurz 1954).

Most discussion of Begram focuses on the material found in two storerooms. Opinions differ on whether these represent a royal treasury or a commercial depot. The caches contain items from all over the ancient world, from the Roman glass to Indian ivories and Chinese laquerwork. On the glass and plaster casts see Menninger 1996, and on the ivories the database and analysis of Mehendale 1997 (online at <http://ecai.org/begramweb/>, accessed 19 October 2010). A large number of the finds from the Begram storerooms were exhibited in the exhibition *Afghanistan, les trésors retrouvés / Afghanistan: Hidden Treasures from the National Museum* (Cambon and Jarrige 2006 and Hiebert and Cambon 2008). Several important discussions of the Begram material, its provenance and chronology are contained in *Topoi Orient-Occident* 11/1 (2001), in the section *Begram et les routes commerciales* (Errington 2001; Bopearachchi 2001; Whitehouse 2001; Dussubieux and Gratuze 2001; Pirazzoli-t'Serstevens 2001; Mehendale 2001; Gill 2001; Callieri 2001).

5.3.2 Old Kandahar – Alexandria in Arachosia

Kandahar has a long settlement history, extending at least into the earlier part of the first millennium BC.

Alexander's eponymous 'foundation' there was rather a refoundation or addition to an already thriving city. In the late fourth century BC, Arachosia passed from Seleucid control to Mauryan, and in the first half of the second century BC was part of the territories south of the Hindu Kush conquered by the Graeco-Bactrian kingdom. On written material and languages in Achaemenid, Hellenistic and Mauryan Kandahar, see Chapter 6, Sections 6.2.2.2, 6.2.3.2, 6.3.1.2, 6.3.2.2, and 6.4.2.

Archaeological excavations at Old Kandahar were carried out under the auspices of the British Society for Afghan Studies between 1974 and 1978; work was forced to cease with the Soviet invasion of Afghanistan in 1979. The initial reports of these field seasons are Whitehouse 1978, McNicoll 1978, Helms 1979, and Helms 1982, with fuller publication in McNicoll and Ball 1996 and Helms 1997. Old Kandahar is the name used for the site of Shahr-i-Kuhna, a large ruinfield 3 kilometres to the west of the modern city, which was abandoned in 1738. Because of constraints of time and resources, excavations were restricted to half a dozen or so individual areas within the much larger ruinfield.

Little or no material among the ceramics and small finds is overtly 'Greek' in the sense of representing direct connections with the Greek world to the west, although excavators found a few sherds of pottery which were probable imports. The initial reports cautiously argue that, while the ceramic and numismatic records reveal connections with other sites in the wider region, both inside and outside nominal Greek control, it is equally important to emphasise the extent to which Old Kandahar did not undergo any revolutionary change in material culture with the transition from Achaemenid, to Seleucid, to Mauryan, to Graeco-Bactrian rule.

Fussman 1966 is an important earlier discussion of ancient Kandahar, and makes hypotheses about the Hellenistic period occupation of the city. Scerrato 1980 discusses funerary material of a later date. More generally on Arachosia, see Vogelsang 1985, Bernard 2005 and Mairs 2010b.

5.3.3 Gandhāra and Northwestern India

The 'Indo-Greek' period in the northwestern part of the Indian Subcontinent dates from the first part of the second century BC, with the Graeco-Bactrian conquests, through into the first century BC and, in some parts of the Panjab, possibly as late as the first part of the first century AD. My discussion will be restricted to this period, and to those parts of the North-West which have yielded evidence, archaeological or numismatic, of political control by Indo-Greek kings. The following section, on India proper, will cover the far less substantial evidence for Indo-Greek military and diplomatic presence into the Indo-Gangetic plain of northern India.

For the wider historical and geographical context of the Indo-Greek remains of Gandhāra and the North-West, good starting points are Allchin, et al. 1995, and the Early

Historic sections of Chakrabarti 1995b; Wheeler 1968 is an older account. On archaeological evidence for the Achaemenid presence in Northwestern India, see Dittmann 1984, and more recently Magee, et al. 2005, Petrie and Magee 2007 and Petrie, et al. 2008 (for further information and bibliography, see the webpage of the Bannu Archaeological Project at <http://www.arch.cam.ac.uk/bannu-archaeological-project/>, accessed 30 October 2010). Also of relevance are Vogelsang's various studies on the Achaemenid East (Vogelsang 1985; Vogelsang 1988; Vogelsang 1992). Chakrabarti 1995a includes the North-West in his treatment of the archaeology of post-Mauryan states in the Indian Subcontinent as a whole. Coningham and Manuel 2008 give a useful summary introduction to the region's archaeology, and Callieri 1995 covers the Indo-Greek period in particular. On material of Northwestern Indian origin at Ai Khanoum and connections between Bactria and the region, see Rapin 1995 and Rapin 1996a.

Gandhāra – Swat – Bajaur: The ancient region of Gandhāra comprises a plain around the confluence of the Kabul and Indus Rivers, with two major urban sites at Taxila and Charsadda, and mountain valleys to the north and north-west (Swat, Bajaur) with important Buddhist remains. Gandhāra historically had close connections to regions to the north-west. It had been part of the Achaemenid Empire, and was on the route of Alexander's campaigns (for an interesting early twentieth-century attempt to trace this route on the ground, see Stein 1929). On Gandhāra's cultural heritage, illicit excavations and the antiquities trade see Ali and Coningham 2002. The Buddhist archaeology and Graeco-Buddhist art of Gandhāra lie largely outside the scope of this survey (but see Allchin 1997 for a collection of useful studies). As in Bactria, many sites which were probably settled under the Indo-Greeks have thus far only yielded material of later periods, or it has been difficult to discern much about earlier occupation under the later strata. Callieri 1995 reviews and provides a useful critical discussion on archaeological material of the period of the Indo-Greek kingdoms in northwestern India, from the time of the Graeco-Bactrian invasions in around 180 BC to the last Indo-Greek kingdoms in the Panjab in the late first century BC or very early first century AD. For earlier archaeological activities in the region, see e.g. Barger 1941 and Faccenna 1964, the latter including accounts of several sites with some material from the last three centuries BC.

The most substantial archaeological evidence for the Indo-Greek presence in the region comes from Bīr-koṭ-ghwaṇḍai (Barikot) in the Swat Valley, with its fortification wall of the second century BC (Callieri 1990a; Callieri 1992; Callieri, et al. 1992; Callieri 1993; summarised in Callieri 1995, 302-304). Significantly, the site also yielded a small number of Indo-Greek coins, as well as terracottas and ceramics with similarities to those of the Graeco-Bactrian kingdom. On imported items and the coins from Bīr-koṭ-ghwaṇḍai, see Taddei, et al. 2004.

In Gandhāran art of later periods the legacy of the Indo-Greeks is plain to see. Of particular note are two schist reliefs depicting the Trojan Horse (Allan 1946; Khan 1990).

See Chapter 6, Section 6.2.3.2, for potsherds and other artefacts from northwestern India with text in Greek characters, and Chapter 6, Section 6.4.2, for Indian Kharoṣṭhī texts containing Greek personal names and official titles.

Taxila: Taxila was the site of three major successive cities, at Bhir Mound, Sirkap and Sirsukh. Sirkap has traditionally been regarded as the Indo-Greek city, laid out in the first half of the second century BC with occupation continuing under Indo-Scythian and Indo-Parthian rule, and Bhir Mound as the earlier Achaemenid and Mauryan city. Sirsukh was founded by the Kushans in the first century AD. Work was conducted at all three sites by Marshall between 1913 and 1934, although comparatively little at Sirsukh, as well as at other monastery and temple sites in the immediate vicinity (excavation reports: Marshall 1951; summary account: Marshall 1960). The results of Wheeler's 1944-1945 training excavation at Taxila remain unpublished. Subsequent excavations have been carried out at Bhir Mound (Sharif 1969; Bahadar Khan, et al. 2002) and Sirkap (Ghosh 1948), as well as surface surveys and excavations which gleaned important evidence on the earliest Taxilan settlement at Hathial, of the third millennium BC (Allchin 1982; Khan 1983). There were also Neolithic sites in the vicinity.

The Bhir Mound = Achaemenid-Mauryan vs. Sirkap = Indo-Greek equation is only broadly accurate. The regular grid-plan of Sirkap, surrounded by a fortification wall, has tended to be viewed as an innovation of the Indo-Greeks, a typically-Hellenic contrast to the 'irregular', or more organic, layout of Bhir Mound. The excavated strata at Sirkap, however, date to later periods, and any artefacts of the Indo-Greek period are 'heirlooms'. Although it may be hypothesised that Indo-Scythian and Indo-Parthian Sirkap maintained the street-plan of the earlier city, the architecture and urban layout of the Indo-Greek city remain essentially unexplored. It is also likely that the settlement at Bhir Mound was not utterly abandoned with the Indo-Greek conquest, but remained in occupation (these chronological issues are discussed in Callieri 1995, 294-297; on problems in the chronologies proposed by excavators, pre- and post- the availabililty of radiocarbon dating, see also Allchin 1993, 69-70, and Dar 1993).

Erdösy 1990, Allchin 1993, Fussman 1993b, and Coningham and Edwards 1997-98 discuss various issues pertaining to the urban layout, chronology and geographical position of Taxila. On its relations with Central Asia and with the western world in general, see Dar 1984 and Fussman 1993b. The temples around Sirkap are treated in Dar 1980; see, in particular, Rapin 1995 on the Jaṇḍiāl 'C' temple, which may date back to the second century BC.

On written material, in Greek, Aramaic and Prākrit, from Taxila, see Chapter 6, Sections 6.2.3.2: Taxila - Sirkap, 6.3.1.2: Taxila - Sirkap and 6.4.2. Taxila was also the place of origin of Heliodoros of the Besnagar inscription (Section 6.4.2), at which time it was under the rule of Antialkidas.

Charsadda: Charsadda, ancient Pushkalavati/Peukelaotis, lies near the junction of the Kabul and Swat Rivers in the alluvial plain of the Vale of Peshawar. The Bala Hisar, a mound some twenty metres high, was excavated by Wheeler in 1958 (Wheeler 1962; see also Wheeler 1968) and from 1993-2000 by a British-Pakistani joint project (Coningham and Ali 2007; preliminary report: Ali, et al. 1997-98; Charsadda (Pakistan) Project: The Bala Hisar: <http://www.dur.ac.uk/arch.projects/charsadda/>, accessed 30 October 2010). More recent research at the Bala Hisar has been carried out by the Pushkalavati Archaeological Research Project-UK (<http://www.arch.cam.ac.uk/pushkalavati/>, accessed 30 October 2010).

At Charsadda as at other sites in Gandhāra there has been, broadly speaking, a tendency to move away from an insistence on Achaemenid control and western influence towards greater emphasis on the local material culture context and pre-Achaemenid settlement. It should be noted in particular that Wheeler's absolute chronology has now been effectively overturned – although his relative chronological framework remains more secure – which has implications for other sites in the region where the excavators dated their analogous finds according to Wheeler's periodisation. Wheeler viewed the Bala Hisar as a Persian foundation and identified a large ditch and wall as defences erected against the army of Alexander the Great in 327 BC. The British-Pakistani Charsadda Project, however, have been able to use radiocarbon dating to establish that the mound was already occupied by c. 1400 BC. Charsadda may thus be recast as an important regional centre, not a Persian colonial outpost, with strong affinities in material culture both with the valleys to the north, and with northern India. For this reason, the introductory chapters to the most recent report on the Bala Hisar (Coningham and Ali 2007) should be consulted before reading Wheeler's 1962 report: these provide an invaluable account of the site's history, previous archaeological excavations, and attendant methodological and chronological issues

A further mound in the vicinity, around one kilometre from the Bala Hisar at Shaikhan Dheri, has been subject to only limited archaeological investigation (Wheeler 1962; Dani 1965/6). It was fortified, and aerial photographs revealed a grid plan which Wheeler compared to the similar regularly-planned city at Sirkap, Taxila (see above). Finds of Indo-Greek coins, and the fact that the lowest levels excavated by Dani stood on alluvial soil, support the thesis that Shaikhan Dheri represents a refoundation by the Indo-Greeks in the first century BC. Occupation at the site continued into the Kushan period.

5.3.4 India

There is, to all intents and purposes, no archaeological evidence of a culturally-distinct Indo-Greek presence further into northern India than Taxila. For contemporary Indian urban sites, see Chakrabarti 1995b. The Indo-Greek (Yavana) invasions of the second century BC are known only from scattered and often cryptic references in Indian and Greek literary and historical sources (evidence and previous scholarship summarised in Wojtilla 2000). The Indian evidence, at least, suggests that the Indo-Greek occupation in the Ganges valley was limited in duration. More generally on Yavanas in Indian sources of this and later periods, see Ray 1988 and Karttunen 1994. Karttunen 1997 provides the best and most comprehensive discussion of relations between the Graeco-Bactrian and Indo-Greek kingdoms and the rest of the Indian Subcontinent, as well as relations between India and the Hellenistic world in general.

Sagala (modern Sialkot in the Panjab) was the capital of Menander in the mid-second century BC. It is described in the later Pāli Buddhist text the *Milindapañha* or 'Questions of King Milinda' (Rhys-Davids 1890), in which Menander debates with an Indian sage, but no archaeological investigation of the ancient city appears to have been undertaken. Bopearachchi 1992 considers the literary and numismatic evidence; Fleet 1905 is an older account.

The former Mauryan capital at Pāṭaliputra (modern Patna in Bihar, Greek Palibothra: e.g. Strabo XV 1, 28) was besieged by the Indo-Greeks, but not, it seems, occupied for any extended period. On the city's archaeology, see concisely Chakrabarti 1995b, 209-212. The positioning of the modern city directly over the remains of the ancient one and the high water table make archaeological excavation effectively impossible. A proposed inscription of Menander at Reh in the Ganges valley (Chapter 6, Section 6.4.2) is in fact nothing of the sort.

On the pillar inscription of the Greek ambassador Heliodoros, from Taxila, at Besnagar, see also Chater 6, Section 6.4.2.

CHAPTER 6
LANGUAGES AND TEXTS

6.1 Overview

The very small amount of textual material recovered from the Hellenistic Far East means that it is impossible to undertake sociolinguistic studies of the depth possible for other regions of the Hellenistic world, such as Egypt. The more limited potential of the Central Asian corpus in Aramaic, Greek and Bactrian for examining sociolinguistic questions, and questions of language and politics, is discussed in Chapter 3, Section 3.2.6. Greek predominates in the epigraphic record: the inscriptions from the sites of Ai Khanoum, Zhiga-tepe, Dil'berdzhin, Takht-i Sangin, Kuliab and Old Kandahar have been noted in the relevant chapters. The Treasury at Ai Khanoum has also yielded philosophical and dramatic texts (Section 6.2.4.1). Greek documentary texts are restricted to the economic texts on jars from the Ai Khanoum Treasury (Section 6.2.3.1), as well as similar, much more fragmentary such texts from other sites (ibid.), and a couple of documents on skin which have emerged onto the antiquities market and are without firm provenance (Section 6.2.4.1: Unprovenanced). There was doubtless a Greek documentary record similar in nature, if not in extent, to the papyrological record from Egypt, but these are the only fragments which have so far come to light.

The presence of Aramaic in the region has long been known from the Aramaic versions of the Aśokan Edicts erected in the mid-third century BC at Kandahar and in Laghman Province in eastern Afghanistan (Section 6.3.1.2: Laghman), as well as an ostrakon from Ai Khanoum bearing text in the Aramaic script (Section 3.2.1: Ai Khanoum). To these may now be added a substantial body of documentary texts in Aramaic (Section 6.3.3.1), from Bactria and dating to the Achaemenid period, allowing us to glean much information about the administration, religious life and ethnic make-up of the Achaemenid Upper Satrapies.

The language of the Kushans was written in Greek characters, and some knowledge of the Greek language seems to have persisted in this period, both as a fossilised register on coin legends, and in the linguistic repertoire of at least one technician who carved Kushan royal inscriptions (Section 6.4.3). Of the local Iranian languages spoken in the region before Bactrian was first recorded in writing, we have only the evidence of names (Grenet 1983).

6.2 Greek

6.2.1 Corpora, Bibliographies and General Works

The Greek epigraphic corpus from the HFE (i.e. all texts not written on perishable materials) is collected in Canali De Rossi 2004 Nos. 285-413 = Chapters IX – XI. These chapters, it should be noted, include some inscriptions which relate to the Hellenistic Far East but were not discovered there, and many 'epigraphic texts' (especially from India) known only from quotation in literary sources: caveat lector. Canali de Rossi's Chapter VIII on Hyrcania and Parthia and the early part of Chapter IX on Drangiana present material from regions adjoining the Hellenistic Far East as here defined. Several items of uncertain provenance, acquired by private collectors through the antiquities market, which bear Greek text came probably from the Hellenistic Far East: these include a silver vessel with an indication of weight (Canali De Rossi 2004, No. 445: Pfrommer 1993, 198; Bernard and Inagaki 2000, 1425); two gold bracelets, one with a weight-mark, the other with a maker's signature; another piece of gold jewellery depicting a female figure with the caption 'goddess' (Canali De Rossi 2004, Nos. 446-448: Bopearachchi and Bernard 2002); and an Achaemenid torque with Greek weight-mark (Bernard and Inagaki 2000; cf. Miho Museum 2002, 207-210). The two Greek inscriptions first published in Bernard, Pinault and Rougemont 2004 are not included in Canali de Rossi's compendium. The volume of the *Corpus Inscriptioum Iranicarum* on Greek inscriptions from Iran and points east (begun by Louis Robert, continued by Paul Bernard and Jean Pouilloux, and now in the hands of Paul Bernard and Georges Rougemont) is to be anticipated with some eagerness, not least for its editions of the unpublished funerary inscriptions from Ai Khanoum (Section 6.2.2.1: Ai Khanoum).

Non-epigraphic texts, including texts on ceramics and other durable materials, are included in Canali de Rossi's compendium. Greek documentary texts on perishable materials are at present known only from three examples, first published in Bernard and Rapin 1994 and in Clarysse and Thompson 2007: see Section 6.2.4.1: Unprovenanced, below for additional bibliography.

An earlier, but still very useful, bibliography of inscriptions and other texts from the HFE was presented in *Fouilles d'Aï Khanoum VIII* (Rapin 1992, 387-392). My debt to it will be obvious in what follows, and without it many relevant works would have escaped my notice. Karttunen 1993 provides another overview of the 'Easternmost' Greek written material known at that time. Discussions of the body of textual material from the region include P. Bernard 2002 and the early work of Robert 1968 is still an excellent starting-point.

6.2.2 Stone Inscriptions

6.2.2.1 Bactria

Ai Khanoum: The Greek inscriptions from Ai Khanoum (see Chapter 5, Section 5.2.2) have generated much interest and a sizeable bibliography. Synthetic studies, with discussion of more than one inscription, include Robert 1968; Robert 1973; Vinogradov in Litvinskii,

Vinogradov and Pichikyan 1985, 98-102; and Narain 1987. A Delphic inscription from the Heroon of Kineas, of which only the last few lines are preserved, concludes with an epigram by one Klearchos, stating that he copied the verses at Delphi itself (Canali De Rossi 2004, Nos. 382-384: the edition and discussion of Robert 1968 remains the accepted orthodoxy, although several critical questions on the inscription's dating and the identity of Klearchos are raised by Lerner 2003-2004). Questions of the possible interaction of Greek and Indian ethnical and philosophical thought in the region have been considered by Schlumberger 1972 and Jajlenko 1990, inter alia. At the Gymnasium, two brothers named Triballos and Straton dedicated a statue to Hermes and Herakles (Canali De Rossi 2004, No. 381: Bernard 1973, 208ff; P. Bernard 1968, 417-421; Veuve 1987, 111-112). The largely-unexcavated cemetery has also yielded two very fragmentary Greek funerary inscriptions, yet to be published in full (Canali De Rossi 2004, Nos. 385-386: Bernard 1972, 608, 622-623; P. Bernard 2002, 78-79; a photograph of one inscriptions appears in Bernard, Pinault and Rougemont 2004, 236, Fig. 4; their publication in the series *Corpus Inscriptionum Iranicarum* is signalled by Bernard in Veuve 1987, 112, and again in P. Bernard 2002, 79).

Zhiga-tepe: For the metric funerary inscription from Zhiga-tepe (Canali De Rossi 2004 No. 304), see Chapter 5, Section 5.2.3, above. Although this inscription is in fact on a ceramic plaque, I include it here alongside other formal Greek votive and funerary inscriptions.

Takht-i Sangin: The votive of Atrosokes from Takht-i Sangin has been discussed in Chapter 5, Section 5.2.1 (Canali De Rossi 2004 No. 311; Litvinskii, Vinogradov and Pichikyan 1985). A fragment of a stone vessel from the site also appears to bear a dedication to the god of the Oxus (Canali De Rossi 2004 No. 312: Drujinina 2001, 263-265).

Kuliab (?): One of the two Greek inscriptions published in Bernard, Pinault and Rougemont 2004 (see also Bernard and Rougemont 2003 and Rougemont 2005) is a Greek altar dedication by one Heliodotos to the goddess Hestia in a 'grove of Zeus', for the well-being of the Graeco-Bactrian king Euthydemos and his son Demetrios (I), already described as a 'glorious conqueror', presumably for his well-known military expeditions south of the Hindu Kush. Like the inscription of Sophytos from Kandahar (Section 6.2.2.2), that of Heliodotos is unprovenanced, but is said to have come from Kuliab, around 50 km north of the Oxus in what is now Tajikistan.

Surkh Kotal: The Greek signature of the maker of a Bactrian stone inscription at Surkh Kotal (Canali De Rossi 2004 No. 314) is discussed in Section 6.4.3, and in Chapter 3, Section 3.2.6, on languages in the Kushan period.

6.2.2.2 Arachosia and India

Kandahar: The inscriptions from Kandahar – the Aśokan Edicts (Pugliese Carratelli, et al. 1958; Altheim and Stiehl 1959; Gallavotti 1959; Kosambi 1959; Filliozat 1961; Pugliese Carratelli and Garbini 1964; Benveniste 1964; Schlumberger and Benveniste 1968; Norman 1972; Christol 1983) and the Greek epigram (Fraser 1979; Oikonomides 1980) – have been discussed in Chapter 5, Section 5.3.2, on Kandahar (Canali De Rossi Nos. 290-293).

The provenance of the first of the two Greek inscriptions published in Bernard, Pinault and Rougemont 2004 (see also Bernard and Rougemont 2003 and Rougemont 2005) is also given as Kandahar. This is the epitaph with acrostich of a man named Sophytos, who recounts his family's misfortunes, his education, travels as a merchant, and his triumphant restoration of his family's position and tomb. The original publications devote much discussion to the question of the origin of Sophytos' name (probably Indian), his use of elevated literary language, and the position of Greek in Arachosia of the second century, the probable date of the inscription.

On language, epigraphy and identity in Kandahar of the third and second centuries BC, see Mairs 2010b. For material in Aramaic and other languages, see Sections 6.3.1.2, 6.3.2.2 and 6.4.2.

6.2.3 Texts on Durable Materials (Ceramics, Bricks, etc.) and Graffiti

6.2.3.1 Bactria

Ai Khanoum: Economic texts from the Treasury reveal a different aspect of life at Ai Khanoum to the inscriptions: commerce, administration, and relations between Greek- and Bactrian-named officials or commercial agents (Canali De Rossi 2004, Nos. 322-357: Rapin 1983; Rapin 1992, 95-114). They were almost all written on intact ceramic vessels, the majority in ink, but a smaller number incised post-firing. For the most part, the texts relate to the contents of the vessels, which include coins, olive oil and incense, or to payments between named parties. These comprise individuals with Greek and with local Bactrian-Iranian names: insufficient evidence, as yet, to say much about ethnic relations and identity at Ai Khanoum. Some non-Greek place-names, so far unidentified, are also mentioned, as are Indian units of currency (in addition to drachmas). The best-known text (Canali De Rossi 2004, No 329: Rapin 1983; Rapin 1992) is dated to 'Year 24' of an unnamed king, possibly Eukratides (Bernard 1985, 99-100; Hollis 1996, n. 18 and n. 26; see also Fussman 1980 on evidence for an 'Era of Eukratides'; Narain 1987, 280-282, disagrees). On financial aspects of the texts see Bernard 1979 and Picard 1984, and for Iranian names, Grenet 1983.

A handful of additional texts on glass and ceramic vessels from the sanctuary of the Temple with Indented Niches appear also to have come originally from the Treasury, and a similar vase inscription came from House 1 in the southern quarter of the city (Rapin 1992, 97-98, 103).

Commodities were likewise named in Greek on alabaster vessels from the Heroon of Kineas (Canali De Rossi 2004, Nos. 368-371: Bernard 1973, 101-102: cinnamon and a poorly preserved name) and on a jar from the Arsenal (Guillaume and Rougeulle 1987, 73: honey). Other, very fragmentary or illegible writings in Greek script came from vessels and other objects found in House 1, the Acropolis, the Arsenal, the Gymnasium, the Propylaea, and elsewhere (Canali De Rossi 2004, Nos. 358-359, 363-367, 372-380: listed, with their inventory numbers, in Rapin 1992, 388).

Burial jars from the Extramural Mausoleum bore names or descriptions of the deceased: 'Kosmas', 'Isidora' and a poignant 'the little one (m.) and the little one (f.)' (Canali De Rossi 2004, Nos. 360-362: Bernard 1972, 618-619; Rapin 1983, 316). See also Section 6.2.2.1: Ai Khanoum, on the unpublished stone inscriptions from the Ai Khanoum Necropolis.

Dil'berdzhin, Emshi-tepe, Tepe Nimlik, Kampyr-tepe, Garav kala: Similar vase inscriptions to the economic texts from the Ai Khanoum Treasury, usually fragmentary but probably containing descriptions of a vessel's contents, its ownership, or payments relating to it, have been found at a good number of sites in Bactria and the HFE as a whole. It is not always possible to date them to the Hellenistic period, and the practice of making such marks in Greek seems to have continued under the Kushans. Dil'berdzhin (Chapter 5, Section 5.2.3) also yielded a couple of ceramic vessels with their contents marked in Greek (Canali De Rossi 2004 Nos. 305-306: Harmatta 1994, 418). Very brief inscriptions of Greek letters, none substantial enough to yield a reading, have been found on ceramics from Emshi-tepe in the Bactra Oasis (Canali De Rossi 2004 No. 302: Rapin 1983, 316; Staviskij 1986, 234), Tepe Nimlik, also in the Bactra Oasis (Canali De Rossi 2004 No. 303: Schlumberger 1947), Kampyr-tepe, on the north bank of the Oxus (Canali De Rossi 2004 Nos. 307-309: Pugachenkova and Rtveladze 1990, 100) and Garav kala, north of the Oxus around mid-way between Ai Khanoum and Takht-i Sangin (Canali De Rossi 2004 No. 313: Staviskij 1986, 264).

Samarkand: The site of Samarkand likewise yielded a few objects – ceramic fragments, bone or baked brick – with Greek letters, including a vase inscribed with the name Nikias (Canali De Rossi 2004, Nos. 387-390: Shishkina 1972, 69; Bernard, Grenet and Isamiddinov 1990, 358-359, 363; Bernard, Grenet and Isamiddinov 1992, 287-289). On similar material from the eastern Iranian plateau, see Pugliese Carratelli 1966.

Kara-Kamar: Found in a cave at Kara-Kamar, above the valley of the Sherabad-darya (Chapter 5, Section 5.2.4) near the present-day border between Uzbekistan and Turkmenistan, were a Greek graffito of the 'N made me' type (Canali De Rossi 2004 No. 310: Ustinova 1990; Rtveladze 1990), and a supposed Latin graffito whose identification as a text of the Roman period is highly dubious (Grenet in *Abstracta Iranica* 13, 1991; Braund 1991; Balaxvancev 1994).

6.2.3.2 Arachosia and India

Kandahar: A few ceramic vessels bore incised or painted Greek letters or monograms, too brief or fragmentary to yield any reading (Helms 1997, 101-102, Catalogue numbers 1983, 1899, 2596, 1402). No. 2596 appeared alongside text in the Kharoṣṭhī script.

Northwestern India: Texts of a few Greek letters similar to some of the briefer jar inscriptions from Bactria have been found in Swat in Pakistan, at Bir-kot (Canali De Rossi 2004 Nos. 295-297: Callieri 1984; Callieri 1990b; Callieri 1990a, 678 and 680) and at Udegram (Callieri 1984, 50-51). A stamp purchased in the bazaar at Peshawar bears a Greek name with patronymic and probable origin on one side, with unidentified, possibly Brāhmī, signs on the other (Canali De Rossi 2004 No. 298: Humbach 1976; see also Section 6.4.2, below). Also purchased at Peshawar was a sardonyx seal with the name Diodoros in the genitive, dated to the first half of the second century BC on palaeographical grounds (Fussman 1972, 24-26).

Taxila – Sirkap: The only non-numismatic evidence of the Greek language at Taxila is a graffito scratched on a terracotta ball found at Sirkap: it appears to be an attempt at writing the word 'Philellēnos', which Marshall suggests may have been copied from a Parthian coin, and thus not contemporary to the Indo-Greek occupation of the city (Marshall 1951, Vol. 1, 41 and n. 4; repeated in Marshall 1960, 23 and n. 1).

Unprovenanced: For the unprovenanced gold jewellery and silver bowl with Greek inscriptions, see Section 6.2.1, above.

6.2.4 Texts on Papyrus and Skin

6.2.4.1 Bactria

Ai Khanoum: Two literary texts, one on papyrus and one apparently on parchment or skin, were preserved as imprints on compacted earth in the Treasury at Ai Khanoum, the original media having disintegrated. Palaeographically, they are strikingly similar to contemporary hands from elsewhere in the Hellenistic world. The papyrus contains a philosophical dialogue in Greek, and dates to somewhere between the mid-third and mid-second centuries BC. Its author is unknown, although several candidates have been proposed, including Aristotle or a member of his school. Images of this, and other texts from Ai Khanoum, may be found on the web pages of Claude Rapin (<http://claude.rapin.free.fr/>). The papyrus was first published in Rapin and Hadot 1987, with an updated second edition of this article in *Fouilles d'Aï Khanoum* VIII (Rapin 1992, 115-121). There have been several re-editions or republications of the text (Canali De Rossi 2004 No. 457: Isnardi Parente 1992; Vendruscolo 1997; Lerner 2003) and it has naturally attracted much further commentary (Bernard 1978, 456-460; Isnardi Parente 1989, 19-20; Berti 1988; La Croce 1989; Crisci

1996, 162-170; Pichikian 1991; 272-273; P. Bernard 2002, 81).

Also recovered from the Treasury at Ai Khanoum, very near to the papyrus and of a similar date, was a Greek text on parchment, published and republished in a second edition by Rapin and Hadot 1987, 249-259, and Rapin 1992, 121-123. It appears in the compendium of Canali De Rossi 2004 as No. 458. Like the papyrus, it was preserved only as an imprint in the earth; the lack of any impression of fibres led the editors to conclude that it had originally been a text on a smooth-surfaced medium such as skin. The text is very fragmentary, but is in verse and may be a dramatic monologue or dialogue.

Kampyr-tepe: The existence of several fragments of papyrus with writing in Greek script from Kampyr-tepe is noted in Rtveladze 1995, 21, but little or no further information seems to be available on these.

Unprovenanced: Three documentary texts on skin have emerged onto the antiquities market, the first pieces of evidence on the Greek administration of Hellenistic Bactria. Like the texts from the Ai Khanoum Treasury, the palaeography of these documents closely resembles contemporary Greek hands from the Mediterranean world, and especially those of Egypt. Although the Ai Khanoum papyrus and parchment might have been imported, these documents now provide evidence that scribal hands in Bactria itself adhered to comtemporary western Hellenistic models. They have also furnished new, and not uncontroversial, evidence, on Graeco-Bactrian chronology, co-regencies and reign lengths. The first text published was a tax receipt (Bernard and Rapin 1994; Rea, et al. 1994; Rapin 1996b); two documents of uncertain genre, possibly a contract and a transaction record, came to light some years later (Clarysse and Thompson 2007). All three documents may have come from the same find-spot, on which see Grenet 1996. Chronological questions arising from the texts, including the light they may shed on a later 'Greek' era of 186/185 BC, known from a Buddhist reliquary (Salomon 2005; Section 6.4.2, below), are discussed by Jakobsson 2009 and Rapin 2010 (available online at <http://claude.rapin.free.fr/Paul%20Bernard%20sbornik2%20-%20Rapin.pdf >, accessed 9 January 2011)

6.2.4.2 Arachosia and India

No Greek texts on perishable materials are currently known from the regions south and east of the Hindu Kush. The only written Greek which appears to have penetrated further into India was that on coins, whether of the Indo-Greek kings or their Kushan successors.

6.3 Aramaic

6.3.1 Stone Inscriptions

6.3.1.1 Bactria

No Aramaic inscriptions are as yet known from Bactria, but see Section 6.3.3.1 below on Aramaic documentary texts from the region.

6.3.1.2 Arachosia and India

Old Kandahar: The only Aramaic inscriptions from the regions south of the Hindu Kush date to the third century BC, the period after Arachosia had passed from Achaemenid control to Greek, and from Greek to Mauryan. These inscriptions have therefore tended to be viewed as the residual survival of an obsolescent imperial register, and assessments of the vitality of this language have varied. As is the case throughout the former Achaemenid Empire, and is certainly the case with the Aramaic documentary texts from Bactria (Section 6.3.3.1), this official or bureaucratic written Aramaic contains many Iranian words. But Aramaic documents from Egypt, too, contain Iranian loanwords, and this is as likely to be the result of the common influence of Old Persian as of the influence of any substantial local Iranian substrate. On Aramaic in Central Asia see Delaunay 1974, and at the various fringes of the Achaemenid Empire, Graf 2000.

The only administrative texts of the Achaemenid period (sixth-fifth century BC) currently known from Old Kandahar are two fragments of a clay tablet in Elamite (Helms 1997, 101: Catalogue numbers 1399 and 1400). It seems likely that these represent the remains of an office of the same sort as that of the Persepolis Fortification tablets (Briant, Henkelman and Stolper 2008; Hallock 1969): the Kandahar fragments are similar in content and physical form. On the implications of this find for our knowledge of the administration of the easternmost provinces of the Achaemenid Empire, see Chapter 3, Section 3.2.6.

Aramaic appears in three separate Aśokan inscriptions at Old Kandahar (Chapter 5, Section 5.3.2): one monolingual Aramaic (Dupont-Sommer 1966; Shaked 1969), one bilingual Greek-Aramaic (Altheim and Stiehl 1959; Filliozat 1961; Pugliese Carratelli, Levi Della Vida, Tucci and Scerrato 1958; Pugliese Carratelli and Garbini 1964), and one bilingual Indo-Aramaic (Benveniste and Dupont-Sommer 1966).

Laghman: Two Aśokan inscriptions in Aramaic are also known from Laghman Province in eastern Afghanistan (I: Henning 1949; II: Dupont-Sommer 1969; Davary and Humbach 1974; Ito 1979). Like the Old Kandahar Edicts, these too contain versions of Aśoka's Pillar or Rock Edicts, and accounts of his religious conversion and decrees to his subjects.

Taxila – Sirkap: A further, brief, Aśokan inscription was found on a pillar re-used in the wall of a later house at Sirkap. See Humbach 1969. The inscription is also included in Dar's compendium of inscriptions from Taxila (Dar 1993, 119).

On the Aramaic Aśokan inscriptions, see in general Mukherjee 1984.

6.3.2 Texts on Durable Materials (Ceramics, Bricks, Seals, etc.) and Graffiti

6.3.2.1 Bactria

Ai Khanoum: an ostrakon with text in Aramaic script was found in the sanctuary of the Temple with Indented Niches (Bernard 1971, 432; Bernard 1972, 631-632; Francfort 1984, 111-112; Rapin 1983, 347-348; Rapin 1987, 59). This findspot may not reflect its actual place of use or manufacture: the post-Greek occupants of the city, for example, are known to have moved material from the Treasury to the Temple sanctuary (see Sections 6.2.3.1: Ai Khanoum and 6.2.4.1: Ai Khanoum, above, on Greek texts). The text appears to be administrative; for a transcription and translation, see Rapin 1992, 105. Because of the lack of grammatical indicators, it is not possible to determine the language of this ostrakon with any certainty. It may be the heavily-Iranianised Aramaic typical of the region, or an early attempt to write a local Iranian language in the Aramaic script.

Oxus Treasure (= Takht-i Sangin?): A gold ring from the Oxus Treasure bears an Aramaic inscription 'to the Oxus' (Dalton 1964 105, Fig. 54, Pl.16). See 6.2.2.1 on the Greek inscription to the Oxus from Takht-i Sangin.

Widemann 1989b publishes a bronze Graeco-Bactrian coin of Euthydemos (late third century BC) with text in Aramaic.

6.3.2.2 Arachosia and India

Old Kandahar: One fragmentary line of Aramaic text is preserved on a sherd from a ceramic vessel (Helms 1997, 101: Catalogue Number 1684). The fabric may be dated to the second half of third century BC, making this text roughly contemporary to the Aśokan Edicts.

6.3.3 Texts on Papyrus and Skin

6.3.3.1 Bactria

The publication of a sizeable corpus of Aramaic documentary texts from Bactria is forthcoming in the series *Studies in the Khalili Collection*, a volume which has been delayed in press for some years (Naveh and Shaked forthcoming). An initial synopsis of the material and its contents is available in Shaked 2004, which aleady contains much useful information. Shaked 2003 discusses toponyms in the documents. The texts date for the most part to the fourth century BC, and provide an invaluable new source of evidence on the administration and ethno-cultural landscape of Achaemenid Bactria, as well as a possible model or point of comparison for the Greek administration of the region, currently known from only a small handful of documents. The position of Aramaic as a regional lingua franca, both before and after the conquests of Alexander, is a question which this newly-discovered material should do much to clarify. As was noted above, the Aramaic material of the Hellenistic period itself is too sparse and ambiguous to permit any insights into language use and language change in the Hellenistic Far East. A common feature, also in the evidence in the documentary material, is the penetration of Iranian vocabulary into the region's written Aramaic. But, as noted above, Iranian loanwords of Persian origin occur in Imperial Aramaic throughout the former Achaemenid Empire. We should therefore be cautious in tracing the influence of any local Iranian languages in the Aramaic of Bactria.

6.3.3.2 Arachosia and India

No Aramaic texts on perishable materials are currently known from the regions south and east of the Hindu Kush.

6.4 Other Languages (Prākit, Bactrian, Unidentified)

6.4.1 Unidentified

A inscription in runic characters on a silver ingot dates to the period after the first destruction level at Ai Khanoum (Bernard, Garczinski, Guillaume, Grenet, Ghassoulli, Leriche, Liger, Rapin, Rougeulle, Thoraval, Valence and Veuve 1980, 27-29; P. Bernard 1980, 439; Rapin 1992, 139-142). Although parallels may be traced with similar runic texts from elsewhere in Central Asia, the script remains undeciphered.

6.4.2 Prākit / Middle Indo-Aryan

On the bilingual Indo-Aramaic inscription from Kandahar, see Benveniste and Dupont-Sommer 1966 and also Section 6.3.1.2: Old Kandahar, above, on the Aramaic Aśokan Edicts. Dar 1993, 118-122, presents a compendium of Kharoṣṭhī and Brāhmī inscriptions of all periods from the sites of Taxila (see also 6.3.1.2: Taxila – Sirkap, above, on the Aramaic Aśokan inscription from Sirkap).

A small number of items with Prākit inscriptions in the Kharoṣṭhī script from northwestern India contain transcribed Greek personal names or titles (summarised in Callieri 1995, 302, and Karttunen 1994, 330). These are for the most part later in date than the actual Indo-Greek occupation of the region, and attest the continuing use of Greek administrative or other official titles. A Buddhist reliquary from Shinkot in Bajaur bears the name of the Indo-Greek king Menander and is apparently palaeographically contemporary to his rule, in the mid-second century BC (Konow 1947; Majumdar 1937; on Menander see also Bopearachchi 1990b and Fussman 1993a). A later inscription added to same casket, in the first century BC, names an individual with a Saka name holding the Greek title *anagkaios*: with little contemporary evidence for official titles in the region, it is difficult to determine precisely what this title implies. It recurs in the inscription of King Seṇavarma of Oḍi, from Swat, of the first half of the first century AD (Salomon 1986). In both these cases the bearer of the title has a non-Greek name. Another Buddhist reliquary, from Swat, dated to the first half of the first century BC, contains the name Theodoros and the administrative title of meridarch (Konow 1929, 1-4), a title which again recurs in the Seṇavarma inscription (Salomon 1986). Another Kharoṣṭhī inscription containing a Greek name comes from a stone seal from Bajaur of the first half of the first century AD: it names one Theodamas (Konow 1929, 6). *Strategos*, too, appears as an official title on two objects, a silver saucer from Taxila and a reliquary: both post-date the Indo-Greeks and refer to officials who do not bear Greek names (Marshall 1951, 613, 777ff; Fussman 1980, 4, 25, 28ff). On a Greek (*yona*) era, datable to 186/185 BC, in a Kharoṣṭhī inscription on another reliquary of uncertain provenance, see Salomon 2005, with futher discussion by Jakobsson 2009 and Rapin 2010.

On the Gāndhārī Prākit Buddhist documents in Kharoṣṭhī script of the first century BC see Salomon 1999 (the British Library fragments; further pieces are published in the University of Washington Press's series *Gandharan Buddhist Texts*) and the website of The Early Buddhist Manuscripts Project, University of Washington (<http://ebmp.org/>, accessed 30 October 2010).

A Greek stamp purchased in the Peshawar bazaar bears characters on the other side which may be Brāhmī (Section 6.2.3.2: Northwestern India). See Widemann 1989a for two engraved gems purchased in the bazaars of Kabul and Peshawar which bear non-Greek names in Kharoṣṭhī script along with imagery similar to that on Indo-Greek coins; the Kabul gem is also discussed by Srinivasan 2010.

A clay sealing from Mathura (in the modern Indian state of Uttar Pradesh) bears the name of the Indo-Greek king Apollodotos in Brāhmī script. Godbole 1993 identifies the figure depicted on the seal as a Nike, and relates it to the Indian literary evidence (in the *Yuga Purāṇa*) for the Indo-Greek conquests in northern India in general, and of Mathura specifically. See Chapter 2, Section 2.3, for references to discussions of the Indian sources in question, and also Wojtilla 2000. Parasher 1991, 114-126, 140 and 240-241 treats the evidence of the *Yuga Purāṇa* in particular.

The Prākit inscription of a Greek (*yona*) from Taxila named Heliodoros, an ambassador from King Antialkidas, is preserved on a dedicatory pillar the site of ancient Vidisha, modern Besnagar in Madhya Pradesh (Canali De Rossi 2004, No. 409: discussed briefly by Karttunen 1997, 296). Heliodoros also describes himself as a devotee of the god Vishnu. For the text with translation and commentary, the edition of Salomon 1998, 265-266, should be consulted, and for further annotated translations see Burstein 1985, 72, No. 53, and Burstein 2003, 234. The inscription dates to the late second century BC.

The reading of the name of the Indo-Greek king Menander, who became a figure in later Indian historical and religious tradition (Bopearachchi 1990b; Fussman 1993a; on the Pāli *Questions of King Milinda*, see Hinüber 1996, 83-86), in an inscription at Reh in the Ganges valley is creative but fantastical (Sharma 1980; demolished by Mukherjee 1986).

6.4.3 From Greek to Bactrian

Texts in the Bactrian language, which began to be written down in a Greek-derived script under the Kushan dynasty in the first-second centuries AD, lie outside the scope of this handbook. Inscriptions and shorter texts in language, written in its modified Greek alphabet, may be consulted most conveniently by non-specialists in Canali De Rossi 2004 Nos. 314-321. On Bactrian documentary texts, see Sims-Williams 2000 and Sims-Williams 2007, and on personal names in the texts, Sims-Williams 2010.

Language shift, the persistence of an 'Ionian' official written register and its replacement by a new 'Aryan' one, is documented in the Rabatak inscription of Kanishka I (Sims-Williams and Cribb 1996). Nearby, at Surkh Kotal (Schlumberger, et al. 1983; Schlumberger 1961), we can view this change on a more personal level, where a man named Palamedes signs the Bactrian inscription he has carved in Greek (Canali De Rossi 2004 No. 314: Curiel 1954, 194-197; Fraser 1982; Bernard 2001 [2003]). See also the discussion in Chapter 3, Section 3.2.6.

CHAPTER 7
ONLINE RESOURCES

7.1 Updates to the Hellenistic Far East Bibliography

Updates to this survey will be published online at <www.bactria.org> and, for users of Academia.edu, also at <http://oxford.academia.edu/RachelMairs>.

All web links given below are accurate and functioning as of 8 January 2011.

7.2 Portals and Collections of Material

The websites listed here are not specific to Bactria or Central Asia, but still contain much useful material:

- *Achéménet*: <www.achemenet.com> Bibliographies, online publications, research tools and news updates on the Achaemenid Empire.

- *Musée Achéménide*: <www.museum-achemenet.college-de-france.fr/> The history and material culture of the Achaemenid Empire.

- *Kushan History*: <www.kushan.org/> Resources on the Kushan Empire.

- *The Annotated Parthia Bibliography*: <www.parthia.com/parthia_biblio.htm> Includes much pre-Parthian material, and a handy digest of recent publications (currently 2007-2009).

7.3 Publications

As noted in the Introduction, many publications on the archaeology of the Hellenistic Far East, and related topics, are now available through various online portals, or maintain their own websites.

- *Google Books*: <http://books.google.com> Provides access to a number of relevant publications (whether full text or as a limited preview), including: Bayer 1738; Rawlinson 1909; Tarn 1951; Holt 1988; Boyce and Grenet 1991; Sherwin-White and Kuhrt 1993; Harmatta, Puri and Etemadi 1994; Lerner 1999; F. L. Holt 1999; Leriche, Pidaev, Gelin, Abdoullaev and Fourniau 2001; and Holt 2005.

- *Persée*: <www.persee.fr> French scholarly journals, including *Comptes-rendus de l'Académie des inscriptions et belles-lettres*, the *Bulletin de Correspondance Hellénique* and the *Bulletin de l'École Française d'Extrême Orient*; free.

- *JSTOR*: <www.jstor.org> Scholarly journals, mostly English-language, by subscription.

- *История материальной культуры Узбекистана* (*Istoriya material'noi kul'tury Uzbekistana*: *IMKU*): <http://kronk.narod.ru/library/imku.htm> Online table of contents for the Uzbek journal *IMKU*.

- *San'at*: <http://www.sanat.orexca.com/> Online archives of the magazine of the Academy of Arts of Uzbekistan: its scope is more broadly cultural and historical, but has some relevant articles on archaeological subjects, in English and Russian.

- *X Legio*: <http://annals.xlegio.ru/sbo/contens/index.htm> Tables of contents and some full-text articles from Soviet/Russian journals, including *Вестник древней истории* (*Vestnik Drevnei Istorii*) and *Советская Археология* (*Sovetskaya Arkheologiya*).

7.3 Field Projects

The websites of archaeological institutes and field projects listed here are all also noted in the discussion of the relevant sites in the preceding chapters.

7.3.1 Afghanistan

- *Délégation Archéologique Française en Afghanistan (DAFA)*: <www.dafa.org.af> Information on current fieldwork and archaeological/conservation training in Afghanistan.

- *France Diplomatie*: <http://www.diplomatie.gouv.fr/fr/actions-france_830/archeologie_1058/les-carnets-archeologie_5064/asie-oceanie_5069/afghanistan-bactres_14847/index.html> A presentation of the DAFA work at Bactra, mostly a repetition of that available on the DAFA website (previous item).

- *Herat - Areia Antiqua* project of the *Deutsches Archäologisches Institut, Eurasien-Abteilung*: <http://www.dainst.org/>, search query 'Herat'. Reports on excavations in Herat, archaeological survey of the province as a whole, and work at the Museum. See also the related DAFA webpage at <http://www.dafa.org.af/index.php?page=fr_Herat>

7.3.2 Uzbekistan

- *MAFOuz de Bactriane*: <http://jeanbaptiste.houal.free.fr/index.htm> *Bactriane du Nord* website, providing information on excavations at Termez, and other activities of the Franco-Uzbek archaeological mission in Bactria.

- *MAFOuz de Sogdiane*: Information on the activities of the Franco-Uzbek archaeological mission in Sogdiana is available on the *France Diplomatie* website (<http://www.diplomatie.gouv.fr/fr/actions-france_830/archeologie_1058/les-carnets-archeologie_5064/asie-oceanie_5069/ouzbekistan-sogdiane_5579/index.html>) and that of the *École Normale Supérieure* (<http://www.archeo.ens.fr/spip.php?article499>). The latter site also contains separate pages on the excavations at the Iron Gates at Derbent, and at Afrasiab-Samarkand, with bibliographies and a PDF file of Rapin, Baud, Grenet and Rakhmanov 2006.

- *Kampyr-tepe*: <http://www.kampyrtepa.narod.ru/> Plans and photographs of the site of Kampyr-tepe; in Russian.

- *International Pluridisciplinary Archaeological Expedition in Bactria (IPAEB)*: <http://diposit.ub.edu/dspace/> The Expedition's preliminary reports (Gurt, Pidaev, Rauret and Stride 2007; Gurt, Pidaev, Rauret and Stride 2008a; Gurt, Pidaev, Rauret and Stride 2008b) are available through the Digital Repository of the Universitat de Barcelona.

- *Karakalpak-Australian Expedition*: <http://sydney.edu.au/arts/uscap/uzbekistan/index.shtml> Contains an illustrated presentation of the sites, bibliographies and updates on recent discoveries.

7.3.4 Turkmenistan

- *Ancient Merv Project*: <http://www.ucl.ac.uk/merv/> Information on the archaeological activities at Merv, illustrated and with bibliographies.

- *Istituto Italiano per l'Africa e l'Oriente, Archaeological Map of the Murghab Delta*: <http://www.isiao.it/en/attivita-istituzionali/attivita-di-ricerca/centro-scavi-e-ricerche-archeologiche/turkmenistan> Brief reports on the most recent excavation seasons, with bibliography.

7.3.5 Pakistan

- *Bannu Archaeological Project*: <http://www.arch.cam.ac.uk/bannu-archaeological-project/> Principally a listing of the Project's publications, some available online as PDF files.

- *Charsadda (Pakistan) Project: The Bala Hisar*: <http://www.dur.ac.uk/arch.projects/charsadda/> Detailed presentation of the Project's research into the chronology of the site, along with a 'web exhibition' on the history of Charsadda and archaeological fieldwork there, and list of publications.

- *Pushkalavati Archaeological Research Project-UK*: <http://www.arch.cam.ac.uk/pushkalavati/> Brief presentation of research at the Bala Hisar of Charsadda and the 2006 field season.

7.4 Field Archaeologists' Webpages

A number of archaeologists working in Central Asis maintain their own professional webpages, with accounts of their research, bibliographies, online publications.

- Claude Rapin (CNRS-ENS): <http://claude.rapin.free.fr/> Bibliography; information on and photographs of fieldwork in Uzbekistan (MAFOuz: Afrasiab, Derbent, Koktepe, Kindikli-tepe, Zerafshan) and Afghanistan (DAFA, Ai Khanoum), Greek texts from Ai Khanoum; articles on the historical geography of Central Asia (including a useful map and bibliography), Takht-i Sangin and Taxila, and Gandharan palettes; and a PDF file of Rapin 2010, with a table of contexts for Abdullaev 2010.

- Frantz Grenet (CNRS-ENS): Bibliography, with links to full text of some articles; information on and photographs of fieldwork in Uzbekistan (MAFOuz: Afrasiab, Koktepe, Derbent, Sogdian paintings); photographs of Central Asian archaeological sites; audio and video of lecture "Sur les pas d'Alexandre en Asie centrale. Recherches archeologiques a Samarcande" (2002, ENS, Paris); and an outline chronology of Central Asia.

7.5 Museum Collections and Exhibitions

- *Afghanistan, les trésors retrouvés: Collections du musée national de Kaboul, Musee Guimet, 6 décembre 2006 au 30 avril 2007*: <http://www.guimet.fr/tresorsafghans/index.html> Educational website on the exhibition.

- *Afghanistan: Hidden Treasures from the National Museum, Kabul*: <http://www.nationalgeographic.com/mission/afghanistan-treasures/> National Geographic website on the exhibition which toured North America in 2008-2010.

- *Tadjikistan: Votivpraxis im hellenistischen und kuschanzeitlichen Baktrien*: <www.dainst.org> search query 'Baktrien'. Project to document the small finds from the Temple of the Oxus at Takht-

- i Sangin, in the collections of the Academy of Sciences of Tajikistan.

- *Begram Ivories*: <http://ecai.org/begramweb/> An online database of the Megram ivories, with discussion.

7.6 Other Relevant Sites

- *3D reconstructions of Ai Khanoum*: brief descriptions and images at <http://www.archeo.ens.fr/spip.php?article1043>, < http://www.archeo.ens.fr/spip.php?article403> and <http://www2.cnrs.fr/journal/1762.htm>.
Four short animations of the 3D reconstruction of the shrine of Kineas may be viewed on Youtube (<www.youtube.com>, search query 'L'hérôon de Kinéas'). These videos come from Episode 2 of the 2004 NHK-France 5 documentary *Eurasian Empires*.

- *3D reconstruction of the Kushan period fortifications at Termez (Tchingiz-tepe)*: <http://www.archeo.ens.fr/spip.php?article1041>

7.7 Texts

- *Greek Inscriptions*: The inscriptions included in Canali De Rossi 2004's *Iscrizioni dello Estremo Oriente Greco* (*Inschriften Griechischer Städte aus Kleinasien 65*) are available online through the database of the Packard Humanities Institute (<http://epigraphy.packhum.org/inscriptions/>).

- *Literary and economic texts from Ai Khanoum* (on the web pages of Claude Rapin): <http://claude.rapin.free.fr/2Textes_litt_et_inscr.htm> Texts, images and editions, along with relevant bibliography. This site also include the Greek documentary text first published by Bernard and Rapin 1994 and Rea, Senior and Hollis 1994.

- *The Early Buddhist Manuscripts Project*, University of Washington: <http://ebmp.org/> A catalogue of Gāndhārī texts, with transcriptions and bibliography.

- *Indian Epigraphy*: <http://indepigr.narod.ru/index_1.htm> Includes texts of the Indo-Aryan versions of the Aśokan Edicts.

BIBLIOGRAPHY

[...] (1963) *Afuganisutan kodai Bijutsuten - Exhibition of Ancient Art of Afghanistan. (Tokyo, Nihonbashi Takashimaya: 3 Sept. - 15 Sept. 1963; Osaka, Namba Takashimaya: 24 Sept. - 6 Oct. 1963; Nagoya, Sakae-cho Maruei Department Store Co. Ltd.: 19 Oct. - 30 Oct. 1963.)*. Tokyo: Nihon Keizai Shimbun Sha.

[Collectif] (1986) "L'Asie Centrale (Résumé des discussions du colloque)," in Pierre Leriche and Henri Tréziny (eds.), *La fortification dans l'histoire du monde grec : actes du Colloque international La Fortification et sa place dans l'histoire politique, culturelle et sociale du monde grec, Valbonne, décembre 1982*, 425-427. (Colloques internationaux du Centre national de la recherche scientifique 614) Paris: Éditions du Centre national de la Recherche scientifique.

Abdullaev, A. (1979) "Раскопки городища Тамошотепе в 1974 г.," in (eds.), *Археологические работы в Таджикистане XIV*, 123-133. Dushanbe: Akademii nauk Tadzhikskoi SSR. ['Excavations at the site of Tamoshotepe in 1974,' in *Arkheologicheskie raboty v Tadzhikistane*.]

Abdullaev, A. (1994) "Отчет пянджского археологического отряда за 1985 г.," *Археологические работы в Таджикистане* XXV (1985), 171-179. ['Report of the Pyandzh Archaeological Team for 1985,' *Arkheologicheskie Raboty v Tadzhikistane*.]

Abdullaev, K. eds. (2010) *Традиции Востока и Запада в Античной Культуре Средней Азии: Сборник Статей в Честь Поля Бернара - The Traditions of East and West in the Antique Cultures of Central Asia: Papers in Honor of Paul Bernard*. (Институт Археологии Имени Я. Гулямова Академии Наук Республикии Узбекистан - Institute of Archaeology, Academy of Sciences of the Republic of Uzbekistan.) Tashkent: Noshirlik yog'dusi.

Abdullaev, K., and Stanco, L. (2004) "Excavation of Jandavlattepa, Sherabad District and Uzbek-Czech Archaeological Research in the Surkhandarya Region, Northern Bactria," *Circle of Inner Asian Art Newsletter* 19, 3-10.

Abdullaev, K. and L. Stančo (2003) "Djandavlattepa: Preliminary report of the 2002 excavation season," *Studia Hercynia* 7, 165-168.

Abdullaev, K. and L. Stančo (2004) "Djandavlattepa: Preliminary report of the 2003 excavation season," *Studia Hercynia* 8, 156-160.

Abdullaev, K. and L. Stančo (2005) "Djandavlattepa: Preliminary report of the 2004 excavation season," *Studia Hercynia* 9, 273-275.

Abdullaev, K. and L. Stančo (2007) "Jandavlattepa 2006. Preliminary excavation report," *Studia Hercynia* 11, 157-159.

Al'baum, L. I. (1969) "Городище Дальверзин-тепе," *История материальнои культурьи Узбекистана* 7, 49-65.

Alcock, S. E. (1993) "Surveying the Peripheries of the Hellenistic World," in P. Bilde, T. Engberg-Pedersen, L. Hannestad, J. Zahle and K. Randsborg (eds.), *Centre and Periphery in the Hellenistic World*, 162-173. (Studies in Hellenistic Civilization 4.) Aarhus: Aarhus University Press.

Alcock, S. E. (1994) "Breaking up the Hellenistic World: Survey and Society," in I. Morris (eds.), *Classical Greece: Ancient Histories and Modern Archaeologies*, 171-190. (New Directions in Archaeology.) Cambridge: Cambridge University Press.

Ali, I. and R. Coningham (2002) "Recording and Preserving Gandhara's Cultural Heritage," in Neil Brodie, Jennifer Doole and Colin Renfrew (eds.), *Trade in Illicit Antiquities: the Destruction of the World's Archaeological Heritage*, 25-31. (McDonald Institute Monographs.) Cambridge: McDonald Institute for Archaeological Research.

Ali, T., R. Coningham, M. A. Durrani and R. G. Rahim (1997-98) "Preliminary report of two seasons of archaeological investigations at the Bala Hisar of Charsadda, NWFP, Pakistan," *Ancient Pakistan* 12, 1-34.

Allan, J. (1946) "A Tabula Iliaca from Gandhara," *Journal of Hellenic Studies* 66, 21-23.

Allchin, F. R. (1982) "How Old is the City of Taxila?," *Antiquity* 56, 8-14.

Allchin, F. R. (1993) "The Urban Position of Taxila and its Place in Northwest India-Pakistan," in H. Spodek and D. M. Srinivasan (eds.), *Urban Form and Meaning in South Asia: The Shaping of Cities from Prehistoric to Precolonial Times*, 69-81. (Studies in the History of Art 31.) Washington D.C.: National Gallery of Art.

Allchin, F. R., B. Allchin, N. Kreitman, and E. Errington eds. (1997) *Gandharan Art in Context: East-West Exchanges at the Crossroads of Asia*. New

Delhi: Regency Publications, for the Ancient Iran and India Trust, Cambridge.

Allchin, F. R., G. Erdösy, R. A. E. Coningham, D. K. Chakrabarti and B. Allchin (1995) *The Archaeology of Early Historic South Asia: The Emergence of Cities and States*. Cambridge: Cambridge University Press.

Altheim, F. and R. Stiehl (1959) "The Greek-Aramaic Bilingual Inscription of Kandahar and its Philological Importance," *East and West* 10, 243-260.

Asimov et al., M. S. eds. (1985) *L'archéologie de la Bactriane ancienne. Actes du Colloque franco-soviétique, Dushanbe (U.R.S.S.), 27 octobre - 3 novembre 1982*. Paris: Éditions du CNRS.

Askarov, A. A. (1982) "Раскопки Пшактепа на юге Узбекистана," *История материальной культурьи Узбекистана* 17, 30-41.

Audouin, R. and P. Bernard (1973) "Trésor de monnaies indiennes et indo-grecques d'Aï Khanoum (Afghanistan). I. Les monnaies indiennes," *Revue Numismatique* 5, 238-289.

Audouin, R. and P. Bernard (1974) "Trésor de monnaies indiennes et indo-grecques d'Aï Khanoum (Afghanistan). II. Les monnaies indo-grecques," *Revue Numismatique* 6, 7-41.

Azimov, I. (2001) "Essai de reconstruction graphique de la citadelle de Kampyr-Tepe," in P. Leriche, C. Pidaev, M. Gelin, K. Abdoullaev and V. Fourniau (eds.), *La Bactriane au carrefour des routes et des civilisations de l'Asie centrale: Termez et les villes de Bactriane-Tokharestan: Actes du colloque de Termez 1997*, 235-240. (La Bibliothèque d'Asie centrale 1.) Paris: Maisonneuve & Larose; IFEAC.

Bader, A., P. Callieri and G. Khodzhaniyazov (1998) "Survey of "Antiochus' Wall". Preliminary report on the 1993-1994 campaigns," in A. Gubaev, G. Koshelenko and M. Tosi (eds.), *The Archaeological Map of the Murghab Delta Preliminary Reports 1990-95*, 159-174. (Istituto Italiano per l'Africa e l'Oriente. Centro Scavi e Richerche Archeologiche, Reports and Memoirs Series Minor III.) Rome: Istituto Italiano per l'Africa e l'Oriente.

Bagnall, R. S. (1997) "Decolonizing Ptolemaic Egypt," in P. Cartledge, P. Garnsey and E. S. Gruen (eds.), *Hellenistic Constructs: Essays in Culture, History and Historiography*, 225-241. Berkeley: University of California Press.

Bahadar Khan, M., M. Hassan, M. Habibullah Khan Khattak, F. Rehman and M. Aqleem Khan (2002) *Bhir Mound: The First City of Taxila (Excavations Report 1998-2002)*. Islamabad: Government of Pakistan Department of Archaeology and Museums and National Fund for Cultural Heritage.

Balaxvancev, A. S. (1994) "К вопросу о датировке латинских надписей из Кара-Камара," *Вестник Древней Истории* 1991, 124-127. ['On the Dating of Latin Inscriptions from Kara-Kamar,' *Vestnik Drevnei Istorii*.]

Ball, W. (1982) *Archaeological Gazetteer of Afghanistan*. Paris: Editions Recherche sur les Civilisations.

Banerjee, G. N. (1919) *Hellenism in Ancient India*. Calcutta:

Banning, E. B. (1996) "Highlands and Lowlands: Problems and Survey Frameworks for Rural Archaeology in the Near East," *Bulletin of the American Schools of Oriental Research* 301, 25-45.

Baratin, C. (2010) "Le grenier grec de Samarkand," *HAL-SHS (Hyper Article en Ligne - Sciences de l'Homme et de la Société)* Accessed 4 October 2010 at <http://hal.archives-ouvertes.fr/hal-00483708/fr/>,

Barger, E., and Wright, P. (1941) *Excavations in Swat and Explorations in the Oxus Territories of Afghanistan*. (Memoirs of the Archaeological Survey of India 64.) Calcutta:

Barth, F. eds. (1969) *Ethnic Groups and Boundaries: The Organization of Cultural Difference*. Bergen; London: Universitetsforlaget; Allen & Unwin.

Bavay, L. (1997) "Matière première et commerce à longue distance: le lapis-lazuli et l'Égypte predynastique," *Archéo-Nil* 7, 79-100.

Bayer, T. S. (1738) *Historia regni graecorum bactriani : in qua simul graecarum in India coloniarum vetus memoria*. Petropolis [St. Petersburg]: Ex typogr. Acad. scient.

Beljaeva, T. V. (1986) "Археологическая стратиграфия Ленинабада," *Известия Академии Наук Таджикской ССР, серия востоковедение история и филология* 1986, 32-40. ['The Archaeological Stratigraphy of Leninabad,' *Izvestiya Akademii Nauk Tadzhikskoi SSR, seriya vostokovedenie istoria i filologiya*.]

Benveniste, E. (1964) "Édits d'Asoka en traduction grecque," *Journal Asiatique* 252, 137-157.

Benveniste, E. and A. Dupont-Sommer (1966) "Une inscription indo-araméenne d'Asoka provenant de Kandahar," *Journal Asiatique* 254, 437-465.

Bernard, P. (1966) "Première campagne de fouilles d'Aï Khanoum," *Comptes-rendus de l'Académie des inscriptions et belles-lettres* 127-133.

Bernard, P. (1967a) "Ai Khanoum on the Oxus: A Hellenistic City in Central Asia," *Proceedings of the British Academy* 53, 71-95.

Bernard, P. (1967b) "Deuxième campagne de fouilles d'Aï Khanoum," *Comptes-rendus de l'Académie des inscriptions et belles-lettres* 306-324.

Bernard, P. (1968) "Chapiteaux corinthiens hellénistiques d'Asie centrale découverts a Aï Khanoum," *Syria* 45, 111-151.

Bernard, P. (1968) "Troisième campagne de fouilles d'Aï Khanoum," *Comptes-rendus de l'Académie des inscriptions et belles-lettres* 263-279.

Bernard, P. (1969) "Quatrième campagne de fouilles à Aï Khanoum (Bactriane)," *Comptes-rendus de l'Académie des inscriptions et belles-lettres* 313-355.

Bernard, P. (1970) "Campagne de fouilles 1969 à Aï Khanoum en Afghanistan," *Comptes-rendus de l'Académie des inscriptions et belles-lettres* 301-349.

Bernard, P. (1971) "La campagne de fouilles de 1970 à Aï Khanoum (Afghanistan)," *Comptes-rendus de l'Académie des inscriptions et belles-lettres* 385-452.

Bernard, P. (1972) "Campagne de fouilles à Aï Khanoum (Afghanistan)," *Comptes-rendus de l'Académie des inscriptions et belles-lettres* 605-632.

Bernard, P. (1974) "Fouilles de Aï Khanoum (Afghanistan), campagnes de 1972 et 1973," *Comptes-rendus de l'Académie des inscriptions et belles-lettres* 280-308.

Bernard, P. (1975) "Campagne de fouilles 1974 à Aï Khanoum (Afghanistan)," *Comptes-rendus de l'Académie des inscriptions et belles-lettres* 167-197.

Bernard, P. (1976) "Campagne de fouilles 1975 à Aï Khanoum (Afghanistan)," *Comptes-rendus de l'Académie des inscriptions et belles-lettres* 287-322.

Bernard, P. (1978) "Campagne de fouilles 1976-1977 à Aï Khanoum (Afghanistan)," *Comptes-rendus de l'Académie des inscriptions et belles-lettres* 421-463.

Bernard, P. (1979) "Pratiques financières grecques dans la Bactriane hellénisée," *Bulletin de la Société Française de Numismatique* 517-520.

Bernard, P. (1980) "Campagne de fouilles 1978 à Aï Khanoum (Afghanistan)," *Comptes-rendus de l'Académie des inscriptions et belles-lettres* 435-459.

Bernard, P. (1980) "Une nouvelle contribution soviétique à l'histoire des Kushans : la fouille de Dal'verzin-tépé (Uzbékistan)," *Bulletin de l'École Française d'Extrême Orient* 313-348.

Bernard, P. (1981) "Problèmes d'histoire coloniale grecque à travers l'urbanisme d'une cité hellénistique d'Asie centrale," in (eds.), *150 Jahre Deutsches Archäologisches Institut 1829-1979, Festveranstaltungen und Internationales Kolloquium 17-22 April 1979 in Berlin*, 108-120. Mainz:

Bernard, P. (1982a) "Alexandre et Aï Khanoum," *Journal des Savants* 1982, 125-138.

Bernard, P. (1982) "An Ancient Greek City in Central Asia," *Scientific American* 246, 126-135.

Bernard, P. (1982b) "Diodore XVII, 83, I : Alexandrie du Caucase ou Alexandrie de l'Oxus?," *Journal des Savants* 1982, 217-242.

Bernard, P. (1985) *Fouilles d'Aï Khanoum IV: Les monnaies hors trésors, Questions d'histoire gréco-bactrienne.* (Mémoires de la Délégation Archéologique Française en Afghanistan 28.) Paris: de Boccard.

Bernard, P. (1987) "Le Marsyas d'Apamée, l'Oxus et la colonisation séleucide en Bactriane," *Studia Iranica* 103-115.

Bernard, P. (1990) "Alexandre et l'Asie centrale: Reflexions à propos d'un ouvrage de F. L. Holt," *Studia Iranica* 21-38.

Bernard, P. (1990b) "L'architecture religieuse de l'Asie centrale à l'époque hellénistique," in (eds.), *Akten des XIII Internationalen Kongresses für Klassische Archäologie, Berlin 1988*, 51-59. Mainz am Rhein: Verlag Philipp von Zabern.

Bernard, P. (1994) "Le temple de dieu Oxus à Takht-i Sangin en Bactriane: Temple du feu ou pas?," *Studia Iranica* 23, 81-121.

Bernard, P. (1996) "Maracanda-Afrasiab colonie grecque," in [...] (eds.), *La Persia e l'Asia Centrale da Alessandro al X secolo*, 331-365. (Atti dei convegni lincei 127.) Rome: Accademia nazionale dei Lincei 127.

Bernard, P. (2001) "Ai Khanoum en Afghanistan hier (1964-1978) et aujourd'hui (2001): Un site en péril," *Comptes-rendus de l'Académie des inscriptions et belles-lettres* 971-1029.

Bernard, P. (2001 [2003]) "Onomastique et histoire : les noms Soxrakès et Palamède dans la Bactriane kushane," *Topoi* 11, 283-320.

Bernard, P. (2002) "L'œuvre de la Délégation archéologique française en Afghanistan (1922-1982)," *Comptes Rendues de l'Academie des Inscriptions et Belles-Lettres* 146, 1287-1323.

Bernard, P. (2002) "Langue et épigraphie grecques dans l'Asie Centrale à l'époque hellénistique," in J. A. Todd, D. Komini-Dialeti and D. Hatzivassilou (eds.), *Greek Archaeology Without Frontiers*, 75-108. ("Open Science" Lecture Series.) Athens: The National Hellenic Research Foundation.

Bernard, P. (2005) "Hellenistic Arachosia: A Greek Melting Pot in Action," *East and West* 55, 13-34.

Bernard, P. (2007) "La mission d'Alfred Foucher en Afghanistan," *Comptes-rendus de l'Académie des inscriptions et belles-lettres* 1797-1845.

Bernard, P. eds. (1973) *Fouilles d'Aï Khanoum I (Campagnes 1965, 1966, 1967, 1968)*. (Mémoires de la Délégation Archéologique Française en Afghanistan 21.) Paris: Klincksieck.

Bernard, P., R. Besenval and P. Marquis (2007) "Du "mirage bactrien" aux réalités archéologiques: nouvelles fouilles de la DAFA à Bactres," *Comptes-rendus de l'Académie des inscriptions et belles-lettres* 1175-1254.

Bernard, P. and H.-P. Francfort (1978) *Études de géographie historique sur la plaine d'Aï Khanoum (Afghanistan)*. Paris: Éditions du CNRS.

Bernard, P., H.-P. Francfort, J.-C. Gardin, J.-C. Liger, B. Lyonnet and S. Veuve (1976) "Fouilles d'Aï Khanoum (Afghanistan): Campagne de 1974," *Bulletin de l'École Française d'Extrême Orient* 63, 5-51.

Bernard, P., P. Garczinski, O. Guillaume, F. Grenet, N. Ghassoulli, P. Leriche, J.-C. Liger, C. Rapin, A. Rougeulle, J. Thoraval, R. d. Valence and S. Veuve (1980) "Campagne de fouilles 1978 à Aï Khanoum (Afghanistan)," *Bulletin de l'École Française d'Extrême Orient* 68, 1-75.

Bernard, P. and F. Grenet eds. (1991) *Histoire et cultes de l'Asie centrale préislamique: Sources écrites et documents archéologiques. Actes du colloque international du CNRS (Paris, 22-28 Novembre 1988)*. Paris: Éditions du CNRS.

Bernard, P., F. Grenet and M. Isamiddinov (1990) "Fouilles de la mission franco-soviétique à l'ancienne Samarkand (Afrasiab) : première campagne, 1989," *Comptes-rendus de l'Académie des inscriptions et belles-lettres* 134, 356-380.

Bernard, P., F. Grenet and M. Isamiddinov (1992) "Fouilles de la mission franco-ouzbèque à l'ancienne Samarkand (Afrasiab) en 1990 et 1991," *Comptes-rendus de l'Académie des inscriptions et belles-lettres* 136, 275-311.

Bernard, P., F. Grenet and M. K. Isamiddinov (1996) "Основные результаты узбекской-французской экспедиции на Афрасиабе в 1990-1991 гг," *Общественные науки в Узбекистане* 3-4, 34-42. ['New Results of the Uzbek-French Expedition at Afrasiab, 1990-1991,' *Obshchestbennye nauki v Uzbekistane*.]

Bernard, P. and O. Guillaume (1980) "Monnaies inédites de la Bactriane grecque à Aï Khanoum (Afghanistan)," *Revue Numismatique* 22, 9-32.

Bernard, P. and H. Inagaki (2000) "Un torque achéménide avec une inscription grecque au musée Miho (Japon)," *Comptes-rendus de l'Académie des inscriptions et belles-lettres* 144, 1371-1437.

Bernard, P., G.-P. Pinault and G. Rougemont (2004) "Deux nouvelles inscriptions grecques de l'Asie Centrale," *Journal des Savants* 2004, 227-356.

Bernard, P. and C. Rapin (1994) "Un parchemin gréco-bactrien d'une collection privée," *Comptes-rendus de l'Académie des inscriptions et belles-lettres* 261-294.

Bernard, P. and G. Rougemont (2003) "Les secrets de la stèle de Kandahar," *L'Histoire* 280, Octobre 2003, 27-28.

Berti, E. (1988) "Le nuove ricerche sui frammenti di Aristotele," *Bollettino Filosofico* 22, 39.

Besenval, R. (2001) "Brève notice sur la coopération archéologique franco-tadjike," *Cahiers d'Asie centrale* 9, 277-283.

Besenval, R., P. Bernard and J.-F. Jarrige (2002) "Carnet de route en images d'un voyage sur les sites archéologiques de la Bactriane afghane (mai 2002)," *Comptes-rendus de l'Académie des inscriptions et belles-lettres* 146, 1385-1428.

Besenval, R. and P. Marquis (2007) "Le rêve accompli d'Alfred Foucher à Bactres : nouvelles fouilles de la DAFA 2002-2007," *Comptes-rendus de l'Académie des inscriptions et belles-lettres* 1797-1845.

Besenval, R. and P. Marquis (2008) "Les travaux de la Délégation archéologique française en Afghanistan (DAFA) : résultats des campagnies de l'automne 2007-printemps 2008 en Bactrian et à Kaboul," *Comptes-rendus de l'Académie des inscriptions et belles-lettres* 973-995.

Betts, A. V. G. and V. N. Yagodin (2007) "The Fire Temple at Tash-k'irman Tepe, Chorasmia," in Joe Cribb and Georgina Herrmann (eds.), *After Alexander: Central Asia Before Islam*, 435-454. (Proceedings of the British Academy 133.) Oxford: Oxford University Press for the British Academy.

Bhabha, H. K. (1994) *The Location of Culture*. London: Routledge.

Bilde, P., T. Engberg-Pedersen, L. Hannestad and J. Zahle eds. (1992) *Ethnicity in Hellenistic Egypt*. (Studies in Hellenistic Civilization III.) Aarhus: Aarhus University Press.

Bivar, A. D. H. (1950) "The Death of Eucratides in Medieval Tradition," *Journal of the Royal Asiatic Society* 7-13.

Bopearachchi, O. (1990a) "King Milinda's Conversion to Buddhism: Fact or Fiction?," *Ancient Ceylon: Journal of the Archaeological Survey Department of Sri Lanka* 1, 1-14.

Bopearachchi, O. (1990b) "Ménandre Sôter, un roi Indo-Grec. Observations chronologiques et géographiques," *Studia Iranica* 19, 39-85.

Bopearachchi, O. (1991a) "Les derniers souverains indo-grecs: une nouvelle hypothèse," in P. Bernard and F. Grenet (eds.), *Histoire et cultes de l'Asie centrale préislamique: Sources écrites et documents archéologiques. Actes du colloque international du CNRS (Paris, 22-28 Novembre 1988)*, 235-242. Paris: Éditions du CNRS.

Bopearachchi, O. (1991b) *Monnaies gréco-bactriennes et indo-grecques: Catalogue raisonné*. Paris: Bibliothèque nationale.

Bopearachchi, O. (1992) "Was Sagala Menander's Capital?," in C. Jarrige, J. P. Gerry and R. H. Meadow (eds.), *South Asian Archaeology 1989: Papers from the Tenth International Conference of South Asian Archaeologists in Western Europe*, 327-337. Madison, WI: Prehistory Press.

Bopearachchi, O. (1993) *Indo-Greek, Indo-Scythian and Indo-Parthian Coins in the Smithsonian Institution*. Washington, D.C.: Smithsonian Institution.

Bopearachchi, O. (1994) "L'indépendence de la Bactriane," *Topoi Orient-Occident* 4, 513-519.

Bopearachchi, O. (1998) *Sylloge Nummorum Graecorum: The Collection of the American Numismatic Society. Part 9: Graeco-Bactrian and Indo-Greek Coins*. New York: American Numismatic Society.

Bopearachchi, O. (2001) "Les données numismatiques et la datation du bazar de Begram," *Topoi Orient-Occident* 11, 411-435.

Bopearachchi, O. (2002) "La présence des Grecs en Asie Centrale: nouvelles données numismatiques," in J. A. Todd, D. Komini-Dialeti and D. Hatzivassilou (eds.), *Greek Archaeology Without Frontiers*, 109-126. ("Open Science" Lecture Series.) Athens: The National Hellenic Research Foundation.

Bopearachchi, O. (2007) "Alfred Foucher et les études numismatiques en Afghanistan," *Comptes-rendus de l'Académie des inscriptions et belles-lettres* 1875-1897.

Bopearachchi, O. and P. Bernard (2002) "Deux bracelets grecs avec inscriptions grecques trouvés dans l'Asie centrale hellénisée," *Journal des Savants* 238-278.

Bopearachchi, O. and M.-F. Boussac eds. (2005) *Afghanistan. Ancien carrefour entre l'est et l'ouest. Actes du colloque international au Musée archéologique Henri-Prades-Lattes du 5 au 7 mai 2003*. (Indicopleustoi: Archaeologies of the Indian Ocean 3.) Turnhout: Brepols.

Bopearachchi, O. and P. Flandrin (2005) *Le Portrait d'Alexandre le Grand: Histoire d'une découverte pour l'humanité*. Paris: Éditions du Rocher.

Bopearachchi, O., C. Landes and C. Sachs eds. (2003) *De l'Indus à l'Oxus: Archéologie de l'Asie centrale. Catalogue de l'exposition*. Lattes: Association imago-musée de Lattes.

Bosworth, A. B. (1981) "A Missing Year in the History of Alexander the Great," *Journal of Hellenic Studies* 101, 17-39.

Bosworth, A. B. (1996) *Alexander and the East: The Tragedy of Triumph*. Oxford: Clarendon Press.

Boyce, M. and F. Grenet (1991) *A History of Zoroastrianism III: Zoroastrianism under Macedonian and Roman Rule*. (Handbuch der Orientalistik. Erste Abteilung: Der Nahe und Mittlere Osten 8.1.2.2.3.) Leiden: E. J. Brill.

Bradley, M. eds. (2010) *Classics and Imperialism in the British Empire.* (Classical Presences.) Oxford: Oxford University Press.

Bradshaw, G. (1991) *Horses of Heaven.* London: Doubleday.

Braund, D. (1991) "New "Latin" Inscriptions in Central Asia: Legio XV Apollinaris and Mithras?," *Zeitschrift für Papyrologie und Epigraphik* 89, 188-190.

Briant, P. (1984) *L'Asie centrale et les royaumes proche-Orientaux du premier millénaire (c. VIIIe – IVe siècles avant notre ère).* (Éditions Recherche sur les Civilisations Mémoire 42.) Paris: Éditions Recherche sur les Civilisations.

Briant, P. (1985) "La Bactriane dans l'empire achéménide. L'état central achéménide en Bactriane," in M. S. Asimov and et. al. (eds.), *L'archéologie de la Bactriane ancienne. Actes du Colloque franco-soviétique, Dushanbe (U.R.S.S.), 27 octobre – 3 novembre 1982*, 243-251. Paris: Éditions du CNRS.

Briant, P. (1996) *Histoire de l'Empire Perse: De Cyrus à Alexandre.* Paris: Fayard.

Briant, P. (2002) *From Cyrus to Alexander: A History of the Persian Empire.* Winona Lake, IN: Eisenbrauns.

Briant, P., W. Henkelman and M. W. Stolper (2008) *L'Archive des Fortifications de Persépolis : état des questions et perspectives de recherches.* (Persika 12.) Paris: De Boccard.

Bulkin, V. A., L. S. Klejn and G. S. Lebedev (1982) "Attainments and Problems of Soviet Archaeology," *World Archaeology* 13, 272-295.

Burstein, S. M. (1985) *The Hellenistic Age from the Battle of Ipsos to the Death of Kleopatra VII.* Cambridge: Cambridge University Press.

Burstein, S. M. (2003) "The Legacy of Alexander: New Ways of Being Greek in the Hellenistic Period," in W. Heckel and L. A. Tritle (eds.), *Crossroads of History: The Age of Alexander*, 217-242. Claremont, CA: Regina Books.

Callieri, P. (1984) "A potsherd with Greek inscription from Bir-kot (Swat)," *Journal of Central Asia* 7, 49-53.

Callieri, P. (1990a) "Archaeological Activities at Bīr-koṭ-ghwaṇḍai, Swāt: A Contribution to the Study of the Pottery of Historic Age from the N.W.F.P.," in M. Taddei (eds.), *South Asian Archaeology 1987: Proceedings of the Ninth International Conference of the Association of South Asian Archaeologists in Western Europe*, 675-692. Rome: Istituto Italiano per il Medio ed Estremo Oriente.

Callieri, P. (1990b) "Раскопки итальйанской археологической экспедиции в районе Бир-кот-Гхвандаи (Сват, Пакистан)," *Вестник Древней Истории* 1990, 118-132. ['Excavations of the Italian Archaeological Expedition in the District of Bir-kot-Ghwandai (Swat, Pakistan),' *Vestnik Drevnei Istorii*.]

Callieri, P. (1992) "Bir-kot-ghwandai: An Early Historic Town in Swat (Pakistan)," in Catherine Jarrige (eds.), *South Asian Archaeology 1989: Papers from the Tenth International Conference of South Asian Archaeologists in Western Europe, Musée national des arts asiatiques-Guimet, Paris, France, 3-7 July 1989*, 339-346. (Monographs in World Archaeology 14.) Madison, WI: Prehistory Press.

Callieri, P. (1993) "Excavations of the IsMEO Italian Archaeological Mission at the Historic Settlement of Bīr-koṭ-ghwaṇḍai, Swāt, Swat Pakistan: 1990-1991 Campaign," in A. J. Gail and G. J. R. Mevissen (eds.), *South Asian Archaeology 1991*, 339-348. Berlin:

Callieri, P. (1995) "The North-West of the Indian subcontinent in the Indo-Greek period. The archaeological evidence," in A. Invernizzi (eds.), *In the Land of the Gryphons: Papers on Central Asian Archaeology in Antiquity*, 293-308. (Monografie di Mesopotamia 5.) Firenze: Casa Editrice Le Lettere.

Callieri, P. (1996) "Margiana in the Hellenistic Period: Problems of Archaeological Interpretation," in Enrico Acquaro (eds.), *Alle soglie della classicità : il Mediterraneo tra tradizione e innovazione. Vol. II Archeologia e arte*, 569-578. Pisa: Istituti editoriali e poligrafici internazionali.

Callieri, P. (2001) "La presunta via commerciale tra l'India e Roma attraverso l'Oxus e il Mar Caspio : nuovi dati di discussione," *Topoi Orient-Occident* 11, 537-546.

Callieri, P., P. Brocato, A. Filigenzi, M. Nascari and L. M. Olivieri (1992) *Bīr-Koṭ-Ghwaṇḍai, 1990-1992: A Preliminary Report on the Excavations of the Italian Archaeological Mission, IsMEO.* (Supplemento n. 73 agli ANNALI - vol. 52 (1992), fasc. 4.) Napoli: Istituto Universitario Orientale.

Cambon, P. and J.-F. Jarrige eds. (2006) *Afghanistan, les trésors retrouvés: Collections du musée national de Kaboul.* Paris: Réunion des musées nationaux; Musée national des arts asiatiques-Guimet.

Canali De Rossi, F. (2004) *Iscrizioni dello Estremo Oriente Greco: Un Repertorio.* (Inschriften Griechischer Städte aus Kleinasien 65.) Bonn: Dr. Rudolf Habelt.

Canali De Rossi, F. (2007) *I greci in Medio Oriente ed Asia centrale : dalla fondazione dell'Impero persiano fino alla spedizione di Alessandro Magno (550-336 a.C. circa)*. Roma: Herder.

Canepa, M. P. eds. (2010) *Theorizing Cross-Cultural Interaction among the Ancient and Early Medieval Mediterranean, Near East and Asia.* (Ars Orientalis 38.) Washington D.C.: Smithsonian Institution.

Cartledge, P. and F. R. Greenland eds. (2010) *Responses to Oliver Stone's Alexander: Film, History, and Cultural Studies.* (Wisconsin Studies in Classics.) Madison, WI: University of Wisconsin Press.

Chakrabarti, D. K. (1995a) "Post-Mauryan States of Mainland South Asia (c. BC 185-AD 320)," in F. R. Allchin (eds.), *The Archaeology of Early Historic South Asia: The Emergence of Cities and State*, 274-326. Cambridge: Cambridge University Press.

Chakrabarti, D. K. (1995b) *The Archaeology of Ancient Indian Cities.* Oxford; Delhi: Oxford University Press.

Chakrabarti, D. K. (1997) *Colonial Indology: Sociopolitics of the Ancient Indian Past.* New Delhi: Munshiram Manoharlal.

Chandra, R. G. (1979) *Indo-Greek Jewellery.* New Delhi: Abhinav.

Chichkina, G. V. (1986) "Les remparts de Samarcande à l'époque hellénistique," in Pierre Leriche and Henri Tréziny (eds.), *La fortification dans l'histoire du monde grec : actes du Colloque international La Fortification et sa place dans l'histoire politique, culturelle et sociale du monde grec, Valbonne, décembre 1982*, 71-78. (Colloques internationaux du Centre national de la recherche scientifique 614) Paris: Éditions du Centre national de la Recherche scientifique.

Christol, A. (1983) "Les édits grecs d'Aśoka: Étude linguistique," *Journal Asiatique* 271, 25-42.

Clarysse, W. and D. J. Thompson (2007) "Two Greek Texts on Skin from Hellenistic Bactria," *Zeitschrift für Papyrologie und Epigraphik* 159, 273-279.

Coloru, O. (2008) "Reminiscenze dei re greco-battriani nella letteratura medievale europea e nella science-fiction americana," in Biagio Virgilio (eds.), *Studi Ellenistici XX*, 519-. (Studi Ellenistici 20.) Pisa; Roma: Fabrizio Serra.

Coloru, O. (2009) *Da Alessandro a Menandro: il regno greco di Battriana.* (Studi ellenistici 21.) Pisa/Roma: Fabrizio Serra editore.

Coningham, R. and I. Ali (2007) *Charsadda: The British-Pakistani excavations at the Bala Hisar.* (BAR International Series 1709; Society for South Asian Studies Monograph 5.) Oxford: BAR Publishing.

Coningham, R. and B. R. Edwards (1997-98) "Space and Society at Sirkap, Taxila: A Re-Examination of Urban Form and Meaning," *Ancient Pakistan* 12, 47-75.

Coningham, R. and M. Manuel (2008) "South Asia: Kashmir and the Northwest Frontier," in Deborah M. Pearsall (eds.), *Encyclopedia of Archaeology*, 733-745. Oxford: Elsevier.

Cribb, J. (2005) "The Greek Kingdom of Bactria, Its Coinage and Collapse," in Osmund Bopearachchi and Marie-Françoise Boussac (eds.), *Afghanistan: Ancien carrefour entre l'est et l'ouest*, 207-226. (Indicopleustoi: Archaeologies of the Indian Ocean 3.) Turnhout: Brepols.

Cribb, J. and G. Herrmann eds. (2007) *After Alexander: Central Asia Before Islam.* (Proceedings of the British Academy 133.) Oxford: Oxford University Press for the British Academy.

Crisci, E. (1996) *Scrivere greco fuori dell'Egitto. Ricerche sui manoscritti greco-orientali di origine non egiziana dal IV secolo a.C. all'VIII d.C.* (Papyrologica Florentina, vol. XXVII.) Firenze: Ed. Gonnelli.

Curiel, R. (1954) "Inscriptions de Surkh Kotal," *Journal Asiatique* 242, 189-205.

D'yakonov, M. M. (1950) "Работы Кафирниганского отряда," *Материалы и исследования по археологии СССР* 15, 147-186. ['Work of the Kafirnigan Team,' *Materialy i issledovania po arkheologii SSSR*.]

D'yakonov, M. M. (1953) "Археологичские работы в нижнем течении реки Кафирнигана (Кобадиан) (1950-1951 гг.)," *Материалы и исследования по археологии СССР* 37, 253-293. ['Archaeological Work in the Lower Reaches of the River Kafirnigan (Kobadian) (1951-1951),' *Materialy i issledovania po arkheologii SSSR*.]

D'yakonov, M. M. (1956) *У истоков древней культуры Таджикистана*. Dushanbe: Tadzhikgosizdat. [*The Roots of the Ancient Culture of Tadzhikistan*.]

Dalton, O. M. (1964) *The Treasure of the Oxus*. London: British Museum.

Dani, A. H. (1965/6) "Shaikhan Dheri Excavation (1963 and 1964 Seasons)," *Ancient Pakistan* 2, 17-21.

Dani, A. H. and P. Bernard (1994) "Alexander and his Successors in Central Asia," in J. Harmatta, B. N. Puri and G. F. Etemadi (eds.), *History of the Civilizations of Central Asia. Vol. 2, The Development of Sedentary and Nomadic Civilizations: 700 B.C. to A.D. 250*, 67-98. Paris: UNESCO.

Dar, S. R. (1980) "A Fresh Study of Four Unique Temples at Takshasila (Taxila)," *Journal of Central Asia* 3, 91-137.

Dar, S. R. (1984) *Taxila and the Western World*. Lahore: Al-Waqar.

Dar, S. R. (1993) "Dating the Monuments of Taxila," in H. Spodek and D. M. Srinivasan (eds.), *Urban Form and Meaning in South Asia: The Shaping of Cities from Prehistoric to Precolonial Times*, 103-122. (Studies in the History of Art 31.) Washington D.C.: National Gallery of Art.

Davary, G. D. and H. Humbach (1974) *Eine weitere aramäoiranische Inschrift der Periode des Aśoka aus Afghanistan*. (Akademie der Wissenschaften und der Literatur; Abhandlungen der Geistes-und Sozialwissenschaftlichen Klasse Jahrgang 1974 Nr. 1.) Mainz; Wiesbaden: Akademie der Wissenschaften und der Literatur; F. Steiner.

Dean, C. and D. Leibsohn (2003) "Hybridity and Its Discontents: Considering Visual Culture in Colonial Spanish America," *Colonial Latin American Review* 12, 5-35.

Delaunay, J. A. (1974) "L'araméen d'empire et les débuts de l'écriture en Asie Centrale," *Acta Iranica* 2, 219-236.

Deloria, P. J. (2006) "What Is the Middle Ground, Anyway?," *The William and Mary Quarterly* 63, 15-22.

Deshayes, J. eds. (1977) *Le Plateau iranien et l'Asie Centrale des origines à la conquête islamique : leurs relations à la lumière des documents archéologiques, Paris 22-24 mars 1976*. (Colloques internationaux du Centre national de la recherche scientifique 567.) Paris: Éditions du CNRS.

Dittmann, R. (1984) "Problems in the Identification of an Achaemenian and Mauryan Horizon in North-Pakistan," *Archäologische Mitteilungen aus Iran* 17, 155-193.

Dolgorukov, V. S. (1984) "Оборонительные сооружения Дильберджина," in I. T. Kruglikova (eds.), *Древняя Бактия 3: Материалы советско-афганской археологической экспедиции*, 58-92. Moscow: Nauka. ['The Fortifications of Dil'berdzhin,' *Drevnyaya Baktriya 3: Materialy sovetsko-afganskoi arkheologicheskoi ekspeditsii*.]

Downey, S. B. (1988) *Mesopotamian Religious Architecture: Alexander through the Parthians*. Princeton: Princeton University Press.

Drège, J.-P. and F. Grenet (1987) "Un temple de l'Oxus près de Takht-i Sangin, d'après un témoignage chinois du VIIIe siècle," *Studia Iranica* 16, 117-121.

Driver, G. R. (1957) *Aramaic Documents of the Fifth Century B.C.* Oxford: Clarendon Press.

Drujinina, A. (2001) "Die Ausgrabungen in Taxt-i Sangīn im Oxos-Tempelbereich (Süd-Tadzikistan). Vorbericht der Kampagnen 1998-1999," *Archäologische Mitteilungen aus Iran und Turan* 33, 257-292.

Drujinina, A. P. and N. R. Boroffka (2006) "First preliminary report on the excavations in Takht-i Sangin 2004," *Bulletin of the Miho Museum* 6, 57-69.

Druzhinina, A. (2000) "Предварительные результаты раскопок на городище Тахти-Сангин," *Археологические работы в Таджикистане* 27, 240-261. ['Preliminary Results of the Excavations at the Site of Takht-i Sangin,' *Arkheologicheskie raboty v Tadzhikistane*.]

Druzhinina, A. (2004) "Предварительные результаты раскопок на городище Тахти-Сангин," *Археологические работы в Таджикистане* 29, 131-160. ['Preliminary Results of the Excavations at the Site of Takht-i Sangin,' *Arkheologicheskie raboty v Tadzhikistane*.]

Druzhinina, A. (2005) "Предварительные результаты раскопок на городище Тахти-Сангин," *Археологические работы в Таджикистане* 30, 86-105. ['Preliminary Results of the Excavations at the Site of Takht-i Sangin,' *Arkheologicheskie raboty v Tadzhikistane*.]

Duke, K. (1974) "Пшактепа - памятник культуры северной Бактрии," *Общественные науки в Узбекистане* 12, 36-38.

Dupont-Sommer, A. (1966) "Une nouvelle inscription araméenne d'Asoka découverte à Kandahar (Afghanistan)," *Comptes-rendus de l'Académie des inscriptions et belles-lettres* 440-451.

Dupont-Sommer, A. (1969) "Une nouvelle inscription araméenne d'Asoka trouvée dans la vallée du Laghman (Afghanistan)," *Comptes-rendus de l'Académie des inscriptions et belles-lettres* 158-173.

Dupree, N. H., L. Dupree and A. A. Motamedi (1974) *The National Museum of Afghanistan: An Illustrated Guide.* (Afghan Tourist Organization Publication Number 6.) Kabul: Afghan Tourist Organization.

Dussubieux, L. and B. Gratuze (2001) "Analyse quantitative de fragments de verre provenant de Begram," *Topoi Orient-Occident* 11, 451-472.

Erdösy, G. (1990) "Taxila: Political History and Urban Structure," in M. Taddei (eds.), *South Asian Archaeology 1987: Proceedings of the Ninth International Conference of the Association of South Asian Archaeologists in Western Europe*, 657-674. Rome: Istituto Italiano per il Medio ed Estremo Oriente.

Errington, E. (2001) "Charles Masson and Begram," *Topoi Orient-Occident* 11, 357-409.

Errington, E. A. and J. Cribb eds. (1992) *The Crossroads of Asia: Transformation in Image and Symbol in the Art of Ancient Afghanistan and Pakistan.* Cambridge: Ancient Iran and India Trust.

Faccenna, D. (1964) *A guide to the excavations in Swat (Pakistan) 1956-1962.* (Department of Archaeology of Pakistan and Istituto Italiano per il Medio ed Estremo Oriente.) Roma: Is.M.E.O.

Filliozat, J. (1961) "Graeco-Aramaic Inscription of Asoka Near Kandahar," *Epigraphia Indica* 34, 1-8.

Firasat, S., S. Khaliq, A. Mohyuddin, M. Papaioannou, C. Tyler-Smith, P. A. Underhill and Q. Ayub (2007) "Y-chromosomal evidence for a limited Greek contribution to the Pathan population of Pakistan," *European Journal of Human Genetics* 15, 121-126.

Fitzsimmons, T. (1994) "Ceramics and the Chronology of Dilberdzhin Tepe and Zhiga Tepe (North Afghanistan)," *Zinbun (Annals of the Institute for Research in Humanities, Kyoto University)* 29, 33-60.

Fitzsimmons, T. (1996) "Chronological Problem at the Temple of the Dioscuri, Dil'berdžin Tepe (North Afghanistan)," *East and West* 46, 271-298.

Fleet, J. F. (1905) "Sagala, Sakala; The City of Milinda and Mihirakula," in (eds.), *Actes de 14e Congres International des Orientalistes*, 1-14. Paris:

Foucher, A. and E. Bazin-Foucher (1942/47) *La vieille route de l'Inde de Bactres à Taxila.* (Mémoires de la Délégation Archéologique Française en Afghanistan 1.) Paris: Les Éditions d'Art et d'Histoire.

Francfort, H.-P. (1979) *Les fortifications en Asie centrale de l'Age du Bronze à l'époque kouchane.* Paris: CNRS, Centre de recherches archéologiques.

Francfort, H.-P. (1984) *Fouilles d'Aï Khanoum III. Le sanctuaire du temple à niches indentées. 2. Les trouvailles.* (Mémoires de la Délégation Archéologique Française en Afghanistan 27.) Paris: De Boccard.

Francfort, H.-P. (1985) "Tradition harappéenne et innovation bactrienne à Shortughaï," in M. S. et al. Asimov (eds.), *L'archéologie de la Bactriane ancienne. Actes du Colloque franco-soviétique, Dushanbe (U.R.S.S.), 27 octobre – 3 novembre 1982*, 95-104. Paris: CNRS.

Francfort, H.-P. (1989) *Fouilles de Shortughaï : recherches sur l'Asie centrale protohistorique.* (Mémoires de la Mission archéologique française en Asie centrale 2.) Paris: Mission archéologique française en Asie centrale; Diffusion de Boccard.

Francfort, H.-P. (1993) "Mission archéologique française en Asie centrale (MAFAC)," *Bulletin de l'École Française d'Extrême Orient* 80, 281-285.

Francfort, H.-P. (2001) "La Mission Archéologique Française en Asie centrale," *Cahiers d'Asie centrale* 9, 249-260.

Francfort, H.-P. (2005) "Asie centrale," in Pierre Briant and Rémy Boucharlat (eds.), *L'archéologie de l'empire achéménide : nouvelles recherches*, 313-352. (Persika 6.) Paris: De Boccard.

Francfort, H.-P. eds. (1990) *Nomades et sédentaires en Asie centrale: Apports de l'archéologie et de l'ethnologie. Actes du Colloque franco-soviétique Alma Ata (Kazakhstan) 17-26 octobre 1987.* Paris: Éditions du CNRS.

Francfort, H.-P. and O. Lecomte (2002) "Irrigation et société en Asie centrale des origines à l'époque achéménide," *Annales. Histoire, Sciences Sociales* 57e année, No. 3, 625-663.

Fraser, P. M. (1979) "The Son of Aristonax at Kandahar," *Afghan Studies* 2, 9-21.

Fraser, P. M. (1982) "Palamedes at Bağlan," *Afghan Studies* 3/4, 77-78.

Fraser, P. M. (1996) *The Cities of Alexander the Great.* Oxford: Clarendon Press.

Frumkin, G. (1970) *Archaeology in Soviet Central Asia.* Leiden/Köln: E. J. Brill.

Frye, R. N. (1966) "A Greek City in Afghanistan," *American Journal of Archaeology* 70, 286.

Fussman, G. (1966) "Notes sur la topographie de l'ancienne Kandahar," *Arts Asiatiques* 13, 33-57.

Fussman, G. (1972) "Intailles et empreintes indiennes du Cabinet des Médailles de Paris," *Revue Numismatique* 21-48.

Fussman, G. (1980) "Nouvelles inscriptions Saka: ère d'Eucratide, ère d'Azès, ère Vikrama, ère de Kaniska," *Bulletin de l'École Française d'Extrême Orient* 67, 1-44.

Fussman, G. (1993a) "L'Indo-Grec Ménandre ou Paul Demiéville revisité," *Journal Asiatique* 281, 61-138.

Fussman, G. (1993b) "Taxila: The Central Asian Connection," in H. Spodek and D. M. Srinivasan (eds.), *Urban Form and Meaning in South Asia: The Shaping of Cities from Prehistoric to Precolonial Times*, 83-100. (Studies in the History of Art 31.) Washington D.C.: National Gallery of Art.

Fussman, G. (1996) "Southern Bactria and Northern India before Islam: A Review of Archaeological Reports," *Journal of the American Oriental Society* 116, 243-259.

Gallavotti, C. (1959) "The Greek Version of the Kandahar Bilingual Inscription of Aśoka," *East and West* 10, 185-192.

Gardin, J.-C. (1957) *Céramiques de Bactres.* (Mémoires de la Délégation Archéologique Française en Afghanistan 15.) Paris: Klincksieck.

Gardin, J.-C. (1977) "The Study of Central Asiatic Pottery: Some Reflections on Publication," *American Journal of Archaeology* 81, 80-81.

Gardin, J.-C. (1980) "L'archéologie du paysage bactrien," *Comptes-rendus de l'Académie des inscriptions et belles-lettres* 124, 480-501.

Gardin, J.-C. (1981) "The development of Eastern Bactria in pre-classical times," *Purātattva: Bulletin of the Indian Archaeological Society* 10, 8-13.

Gardin, J.-C. (1982) "Vers une géographie archéologique de l'Afghanistan," *Studia Iranica* 11, 97-110.

Gardin, J.-C. (1984) "Canal Irrigation in Bronze Age Eastern Bactria," in B. B. Lal and S. P. Gupta (eds.), *Frontiers of the Indus Civilization (Sir Mortimer Wheeler Commemorative Volume)*, 311-320. New Delhi: Indian Archaeological Society.

Gardin, J.-C. (1985a) "Les relations entre la Méditerranée et la Bactriane dans l'antiquité, d'après des données céramologiques inédites," in J.-L. Huot, M. Yon and Y. Calvet (eds.), *De l'Indus aux Balkans, Recueil à la mémoire de Jean Deshayes*, 447-460. Paris: Editions Recherche sur les Civilisations.

Gardin, J.-C. (1985b) "Pour une géographie archéologique de la Bactriane," in M. S. Asimov et al. (eds.), *L'archéologie de la Bactriane ancienne. Actes du Colloque franco-soviétique, Dushanbe (U.R.S.S.), 27 octobre – 3 novembre 1982*, 39-45. Paris: CNRS.

Gardin, J.-C. (1986) "Migrateurs et porteurs de pots en Bactriane de l'âge du bronze à nos jours," in M. T. Barrelet (eds.), *À propos des interprétations archéologiques de la poterie*, 79-94. Paris:

Gardin, J.-C. (1995) "Fortified sites of eastern Bactria (Afghanistan) in Pre-Hellenistic times," in A. Invernizzi (eds.), *In the Land of the Gryphons: Papers on Central Asian Archaeology in Antiquity*, 83-105. (Monografie di Mesopotamia 5.) Firenze: Casa Editrice Le Lettere.

Gardin, J.-C. (1998) *Prospections archéologiques en Bactriane orientale (1974-1978) 3: Description des sites et notes de synthèse.* (Mémoires de la Mission archéologique française en Asie centrale 9.) Paris: Éditions Recherche sur les Civilisations.

Gardin, J.-C. and P. Gentelle (1976) "Irrigation et peuplement dans la plaine d'Aï Khanoum, de l'époque achéménide à l'époque musulmane," *Bulletin de l'École Française d'Extrême Orient* 63, 59-110.

Gardin, J.-C. and P. Gentelle (1979) "L'exploitation du sol en Bactriane antique," *Bulletin de l'École Française d'Extrême Orient* 66, 1-29.

Gardin, J.-C. and B. Lyonnet (1979) "La prospection archéologique de la Bactriane orientale (1974-1978): premiers résultats," *Mesopotamia* 13-14, 99-154.

Gentelle, P. (1978) *Étude géographique de la plaine d'Aï Khanoum et de son irrigation depuis les temps antiques.* (Publications de l'URA 10; Centre de

Recherches Archéologiques Mémoire 2.) Paris: Éditions du CNRS.

Gentelle, P. (1985) "Déterminants écologiques de l'irrigation ancienne en Bactriane orientale," in M. S. et al. Asimov (eds.), *L'archéologie de la Bactriane ancienne. Actes du Colloque franco-soviétique, Dushanbe (U.R.S.S.), 27 octobre – 3 novembre 1982*, 159-167. Paris: CNRS.

Gentelle, P. (1989) *Prospections archéologiques en Bactriane orientale (1974-1978) 1: Données paléogéographiques et fondements de l'irrigation*. (Mémoires de la Mission archéologique française en Asie centrale 3.) Paris: De Boccard.

Gentelle, P. (2001) "Irrigations antiques en Bactriane du nord : l'image du satellite, la prospection archéologique, les inférences historiques," in P. Leriche, C. Pidaev, M. Gelin, K. Abdoullaev and V. Fourniau (eds.), *La Bactriane au carrefour des routes et des civilisations de l'Asie centrale: Termez et les villes de Bactriane-Tokharestan: Actes du colloque de Termez 1997*, 163-172. (La Bibliothèque d'Asie centrale 1.) Paris: Maisonneuve & Larose; IFEAC.

Gentelle, P. and F.-M. Le Tourneau (2007 [2000]) "Etude par télédétection de la vallée de Samarcande " *Cybergeo, Actes des Journées de Télédétection en Sciences humaines* article 161, mis en ligne le 5 mai 2000, modifié le 07 mars 2007.

Ghirshman, R. (1946) *Bégram: Recherches archéologiques et historiques sur les Kouchans*. (Mémoires de la Délégation Archéologique Française en Afghanistan 12; Mémoires de l'Institut Français d'Archéologie Orientale du Caire 79.) Cairo:

Ghosh, A. (1948) "Taxila (Sirkap), 1944-5," *Ancient India* 4, 41-84.

Gill, S. (2001) "Procédés narratifs dans les ivoires de Begram," *Topoi Orient-Occident* 11, 515-535.

Godbole, S. D. (1993) "Mathura Clay Sealing of Apollodotus," in Tony Hackens and Ghislaine Moucharte (eds.), *Actes du XIe Congrès international de numismatique, Bruxelles, 8-13 septembre 1991. Vol. 1*, 311-312. Louvain: Association Professeur Marcel Hoc. [Title as printed has a typographical error: 'Appolodotus' for 'Apollodotus'.]

Gorshenina, S. and C. Rapin (2001) *Les archéologues en Asie centrale : de Kaboul à Samarcande*. (Collection Découvertes Gallimard 411, série Archéologie.) Paris: Gallimard.

Gosden, C. and Y. Marshall (1999) "The Cultural Biography of Objects," *World Archaeology* 33, 169-178.

Graf, D. F. (2000) "Aramaic on the Periphery of the Achaemenid Realm," *Archäologische Mitteilungen aus Iran und Turan* 32, 75-92.

Green, A. (2002) "The "Treasure of Bactria" in the Miho Museum," in Miho Museum (eds.), *Treasures of Ancient Bactria*, 220-221. Shigaraki: Miho Museum.

Green, P. (1990) *Alexander to Actium: The Hellenistic Age*. Berkeley: University of California Press.

Grenet, F. (1983) "L'onomastique iranienne à Aï Khanoum," *Bulletin de Correspondance Hellénique* 107, 373-381.

Grenet, F. (1984) *Les pratiques funéraires dans l'Asie centrale sédentaire: de la conquête grecque à l'Islamisation*. (Publications de l'U.R.A. 29; Centre de recherches archéologiques mémoires 1.) Paris: CNRS.

Grenet, F. (1987a) "L'Athéna de Dil'berdžin," in Frantz Grenet (eds.), *Cultes et monuments religieux dans l'Asie centrale préislamique*, 41-45. (Publications de l'UA 1222 (Centre national de la recherche scientifique), Mémoire 2.) Paris: CNRS.

Grenet, F. (1991) "Mithra au temple principal d'Aï Khanoum?," in P. Bernard and F. Grenet (eds.), *Histoire et cultes de l'Asie centrale préislamique: Sources écrites et documents archéologiques. Actes du colloque international du CNRS (Paris, 22-28 Novembre 1988)*, 147-151. Paris: Éditions du CNRS.

Grenet, F. (1996) "Ασαγγωρνοιc, Αckιcαγγοραγο, Sangchârak," *Topoi* 6, 470-474.

Grenet, F. (1999) "Review of Olivier-Utard (1997)," *Bulletin of the School of Oriental and African Studies* 62, 159-160.

Grenet, F. (2004) "Maracanda/Samarkand, une métropole pré-mongole. Sources écrites et archéologie," *Annales. Histoire, Sciences Sociales* 2004, 1043-1067.

Grenet, F. eds. (1987b) *Cultes et monuments religieux dans l'Asie centrale préislamique*. (Publications de l'UA 1222 (Centre national de la recherche scientifique), Mémoire 2.) Paris: CNRS.

Grenet, F. and M. Isamiddinov (2001) "Brève chronique des fouilles de la MAFOUZ (Mission Archéologique Franco-Ouzbèke) en 2000," *Cahiers d'Asie centrale* 9, 237-242.

Grenet, F. and C. Rapin (1998a) "Alexander, Aï Khanum, Termez: Remarks on the Spring Campaign of 328," *Bulletin of the Asia Institute* 12, 79-89.

Grenet, F. and C. Rapin (1998b) "De la Samarkand antique à la Samarkand islamique: continuités et ruptures," in Roland-Pierre Gayraud (eds.), *Colloque international d'archéologie islamique, IFAO, Le Caire, 3-7 février 1993*, (Textes arabes et études islamiques 36.) Cairo: Institut français d'archéologie orientale.

Guillaume, O. (1983) *Fouilles d'Aï Khanoum II. Les propylées de le rue principale.* (Mémoires de la Délégation Archéologique Française en Afghanistan 26.) Paris: De Boccard.

Guillaume, O. (1985) "Contribution à l'étude d'un artisanat bactrien pré-hellénistique," in M. S. Asimov et al. (eds.), *L'archéologie de la Bactriane ancienne. Actes du Colloque franco-soviétique, Dushanbe (U.R.S.S.), 27 octobre – 3 novembre 1982*, 257-267. Paris: CNRS.

Guillaume, O. (1990) *Analysis of Reasonings in Archaeology: The Case of Graeco-Bactrian and Indo-Greek Numismatics.* (French Studies in the South Asian Culture and Society 4.) Delhi: Oxford University Press.

Guillaume, O. (1991) *Graeco-Bactrian and Indian Coins from Afghanistan.* (French Studies in South Asian Culture and Society 5.) Delhi: Oxford University Press.

Guillaume, O. and A. Rougeulle (1987) *Fouilles d'Aï Khanoum VII. Les petits objets.* (Mémoires de la Délégation Archéologique Française en Afghanistan 31.) Paris: De Boccard.

Gurt, J. M., S. Pidaev, A. M. Rauret and S. Stride (2007) *Preliminary report of the first season work of the International Pluridisciplinary Archaeological Expedition to Bactria 2006.* Barcelona: ERAUB.

Gurt, J. M., S. Pidaev, A. M. Rauret and S. Stride (2008a) *Preliminary report of the first season work of the International Pluridisciplinary Archaeological Expedition to Bactria 2007.* Barcelona: ERAUB.

Gurt, J. M., S. Pidaev, A. M. Rauret and S. Stride (2008b) *Preliminary report of the first season work of the International Pluridisciplinary Archaeological Expedition to Bactria 2008.* Barcelona: ERAUB.

Hackin, J. (1939) *Recherches archéologiques à Begram.* (Mémoires de la Délégation Archéologique Française en Afghanistan 9.) Paris: Les Éditions d'Art et d'Histoire.

Hackin, J. (1954) *Nouvelles recherches archéologiques à Begram.* (Mémoires de la Délégation Archéologique Française en Afghanistan 11.) Paris: Imprimerie Nationale-Presses Universitaires.

Hall, E. and P. Vasunia eds. (2010) *India, Greece, and Rome, 1757 to 2007.* (Bulletin of the Institute of Classical Studies Supplement 108.) London: Institute of Classical Studies, School of Advanced Study, University of London.

Hall, J. M. (1997) *Ethnic Identity in Greek Antiquity.* Cambridge: Cambridge University Press.

Hallock, R. T. (1969) *Persepolis Fortification Tablets.* (University of Chicago Oriental Institute Publications 92.) Chicago: University of Chicago Press.

Hannestad, L. and D. Potts (1990) "Temple Architecture in the Seleucid Kingdom," in P. Bilde et al. (eds.), *Religion and Religious Practice in the Seleucid Kingdom*, 91-124. (Studies in Hellenistic Civilization 1.) Aarhus: Aarhus University Press.

Harmatta, J. (1994) "Languages and Scripts in Graeco-Bactria and the Saka Kingdoms," in J. Harmatta, B. N. Puri and G. F. Etemadi (eds.), *History of the Civilizations of Central Asia. Vol. 2, The Development of Sedentary and Nomadic Civilizations: 700 B.C. to A.D. 250*, 397-418. Paris: UNESCO.

Harmatta, J., B. N. Puri and G. F. Etemadi eds. (1994) *History of the Civilizations of Central Asia. Vol. 2, The Development of Sedentary and Nomadic Civilizations: 700 B.C. to A.D. 250.* Paris: UNESCO.

Hasanov, M. (1998) "Об одной греческой находке с городища Нуртепа," *История материальнои культуры Узбекистана* 29, 43-46. ['On a Greek Find at the Settlement of Nurtepe,' *Istoriya material'noi kul'tury Uzbekistana*.]

Helms, S. and V. N. Yagodin (1997) "Excavations at Kazakl'i-Yatkan in the Tash-Ki'rman Oasis of Ancient Chorasmia: A Preliminary Report," *Iran* 35, 43-65.

Helms, S. W. (1979) "Old Kandahar Excavations 1976: Preliminary Report," *Afghan Studies* 2, 1-8.

Helms, S. W. (1982) "Excavations at "The City and the Famous Fortress of Kandahar, the Foremost Place in all of Asia"," *Afghan Studies* 3/4, 1-24.

Helms, S. W. (1997) *Excavations at Old Kandahar in Afghanistan 1976-1978: Conducted on Behalf of the Society for South Asian Studies (Society for*

Afghan Studies). Stratigraphy, Pottery and Other Finds. (BAR International Series 686; Society for South Asian Studies Monograph 2.) Oxford: BAR Publishing.

Helms, S. W. (1998) "Ancient Chorasmia: The Northern Edge of Central Asia from the 6th Century B.C. to the mid-4th Century A.D.," in D. Christian and C. Benjamin (eds.), *Worlds of the Silk Roads: Ancient and Modern*, 77-96. (Silk Road Studies 2.) Turnhout: Brepols.

Helms, S. W., V. N. Yagodin, A. V. G. Betts, G. Khodzhaniyazov and M. Negus (2002) "The Karakalpak-Australian Excavations in Ancient Chorasmia: The Northern Frontier of the 'Civilised' Ancient World," *Ancient Near Eastern Studies* 39, 3-43.

Helms, S. W., V. N. Yagodin, A. V. G. Betts, G. Khozhaniyazov and F. Kidd (2001) "Five Seasons of Excavations in the Tash-k'irman Oasis of Ancient Chorasmia, 1996-2000. An Interim Report," *Iran* 39, 119-144.

Henning, W. B. (1949) "The Aramaic Inscription of Asoka Found in Lampāka," *Bulletin of the School of Oriental and African Studies* 13, 80-88.

Herrmann, G. and K. Kurbansakhatov (1995) "The International Merv Project Preliminary Report on the Third Season (1994)," *Iran* 33, 31-60.

Herrmann, G., K. Kurbansakhatov and e. al. (1994) "The International Merv Project Preliminary Report on the Second Season (1993)," *Iran* 32, 53-75.

Herrmann, G., K. Kurbansakhatov and S. J. Simpson (1996) "The International Merv Project Preliminary Report on the Fourth Season (1995)," *Iran* 34, 1-22.

Herrmann, G., K. Kurbansakhatov and S. J. Simpson (1997) "The International Merv Project Preliminary Report on the Fifth Season (1996)," *Iran* 35, 1-33.

Herrmann, G., K. Kurbansakhatov and S. J. Simpson (1998) "The International Merv Project. Preliminary Report on the Sixth Season (1997)," *Iran* 36, 53-75.

Herrmann, G., K. Kurbansakhatov and S. J. Simpson (1999) "The International Merv Project. Preliminary Report on the Seventh Season (1998)," *Iran* 37, 1-24.

Herrmann, G., K. Kurbansakhatov and S. J. Simpson (2000) "The International Merv Project. Preliminary Report on the Eighth Season (1999)," *Iran* 38, 1-31.

Herrmann, G., K. Kurbansakhatov and S. J. Simpson (2001) "The International Merv Project. Preliminary Report on the Ninth Year (2000)," *Iran* 39, 9-52.

Herrmann, G., V. M. Masson and K. Kurbansakhatov (1993) "The International Merv Project Preliminary Report on the First Season (1992)," *Iran* 31, 39-62.

Hiebert, F. and P. Cambon eds. (2008) *Afghanistan: Hidden Treasures from the National Museum, Kabul*. Washingon, D.C.: National Geographic.

Hinüber, O. v. (1996) *A Handbook of Pāli Literature*. (Indian Philology and South Asian Studies 2.) Berlin: Walter de Gruyter.

Hollis, A. S. (1996) "Laodice Mother of Eucratides of Bactria," *Zeitschrift für Papyrologie und Epigraphik* 110, 161-164.

Holt, F. L. (1981) "The Euthydemid Coinage of Bactria: Further Hoard Evidence from Ai Khanoum," *Revue Numismatique* 6, 7-44.

Holt, F. L. (1987) "Hellenistic Bactria: Beyond the Mirage," *Ancient World* 15, 3-15.

Holt, F. L. (1988) *Alexander the Great and Bactria: The Formation of a Greek Frontier in Central Asia*. (Mnemosyne, bibliotheca classica Batava. Supplementum 104) Leiden; New York: E. J. Brill.

Holt, F. L. (1999) *Thundering Zeus: The Making of Hellenistic Bactria*. (Hellenistic Culture and Society XXXII.) Berkeley: University of California Press.

Holt, F. L. (2003) *Alexander the Great and the Mystery of the Elephant Medallions*. (Hellenistic Culture and Society 44.) Berkeley: University of California Press.

Holt, F. L. (2005) *Into the Land of Bones: Alexander the Great in Afghanistan*. (Hellenistic Culture and Society 47.) Berkeley: University of California Press.

Holt, T. (1999) *Alexander at the World's End*. London: Abacus.

Horner, I. B. (1963-4) *Milinda's Questions*. Bristol: Pali Text Society.

Huff, D., C. Pidaev and C. Chaydoullaev (2001) "Uzbek-German archaeological researches in the Surkhan Darya region," in P. Leriche, C. Pidaev, M. Gelin, K. Abdoullaev and V. Fourniau (eds.), *La Bactriane au carrefour des routes et des civilisations de l'Asie centrale: Termez et les* villes de Bactriane-Tokharestan: Actes du colloque de Termez 1997, 219-233. (La Bibliothèque d'Asie centrale 1.) Paris: Maisonneuve & Larose; IFEAC.

Humbach, H. (1969) *Die aramäische Inschrift von Taxila*. (Abhandlungen der Geistes- und Sozialwissenschaftlichen Klasse; Akademie der Wissenschaften und der Literatur; Abhandlungen der Geistes-und Sozialwissenschaftlichen Klasse.) Mainz; Stuttgart: Akademie der Wissenschaften und der Literatur; F. Steiner.

Humbach, H. (1976) "Eine griechische Inschrift aus Pakistan," *Gutenberg-Jahrbuch* 1976, 15-17.

Inevatkina, O. N. (2002) "Фортификатсия акрополя древнего Самарканда в середине первого тысыячелетия до н.е.," *Материальная культура Востока* 3, 24-46. ['The fortification of the acropolis of ancient Samarkand in the middle of the 1st millennium B.C.E.,' *Material'naya kul'tura Vostoka*.]

Invernizzi, A. (1995a) "Corinthian terracotta assembled capitals in Hellenistic Asia," in A. Invernizzi (eds.), *In the Land of the Gryphons: Papers on Central Asian Archaeology in Antiquity*, 3-12. (Monografie di Mesopotamia 5.) Firenze: Casa Editrice Le Lettere.

Invernizzi, A. eds. (1995b) *In the Land of the Gryphons: Papers on Central Asian Archaeology in Antiquity*. Firenze: Casa Editrice Le Lettere.

Isamiddinov, M. (2010) "Stratigraphy of the Koktepa Site and Certain Aspects of History and Culture of Sogdia in the Hellenistic Period," in Kazim Abdullaev (eds.), *Традиции Востока и Запада в Античной Культуре Средней Азии: Сборник Статей в Честь Поля Бернара - The Traditions of East and West in the Antique Cultures of Central Asia: Papers in Honor of Paul Bernard*, 131-140. (Институт Археологии Имени Я. Гулямова Академии Наук Республикии Узбекистан - Institute of Archaeology, Academy of Sciences of the Republic of Uzbekistan.) Tashkent: Noshirlik yog'dusi.

Isnardi Parente, M. (1989) *L'eredità di Platone nell'Accademia antica*. (Istituto italiano per gli studi filosofici. Saggi, 5.) Milano: Edizioni Angelo Guerini e Associati.

Isnardi Parente, M. (1992) "Il papiro filosofico di Aï Khanoum," in Antonio Carlini and et al. (eds.), *Studi su codici e papiri filosofici. Platone, Aristotele, Ierocle*, 169-188. (Studi e testi per il Corpus dei papiri filosofici greci e latini 6; Studi (Accademia toscana di scienze e lettere La Colombaria) 129.) Firenze: Leo S. Olschki Editore.

Ito, G. (1979) "Aśokan Inscriptions, Laghmân I and II," *Studia Iranica* 8, 175-183.

Jairazbhoy, R. A. (1963) *Foreign Influence in Ancient India*. Bombay: Asia Publishing House.

Jajlenko, V. P. (1990) "Les maximes delphiques d'Aï Khanoum et la formation de la doctrine du *Dhamma* d'Asoka," *Dialogues d'histoire ancienne* 16, 239-256.

Jakobsson, J. (2009) "Who founded the Indo-Greek era of 186/185 B.C.E.?," *Classical Quarterly* 59, 505-510.

Jamroziak, W. (1978) "The Historical SF of Teodor Parnicki," *Science Fiction Studies* 5, 130-133.

Jarrige, J.-F. (1985) "Les relations entre l'Asie centrale méridionale, le Baluchistan et la vallée de l'Indus à la fin du 3e et au début du 2e millénaire," in M. S. et al. Asimov (eds.), *L'archéologie de la Bactriane ancienne. Actes du Colloque franco-soviétique, Dushanbe (U.R.S.S.), 27 octobre – 3 novembre 1982*, 106-118. Paris: CNRS.

Jones, S. (1998) *The Archaeology of Ethnicity: Constructing Identities in the Past and Present*. London: Routledge.

Karttunen, K. (1989) *India in Early Greek Literature*. (Studia Orientalia 65.) Helsinki: Finnish Oriental Society.

Karttunen, K. (1993) "Easternmost Greek Epigraphy," in A. J. Gail and G. J. R. Mevissen (eds.), *South Asian Archaeology 1991*, 493-500. Berlin:

Karttunen, K. (1994) "Yonas, Yavanas, and related matter in Indian Epigraphy," in A. Parpola and P. Koskikallio (eds.), *South Asian Archaeology 1993: Proceedings of the Twelfth International Conference of the European Association of South Asian Archaeologists*, 329-336. (Annales Academiae Scientiarum Fennicae B 271.) Helsinki: Suomalainen Tiedeakatemia.

Karttunen, K. (1997) *India and the Hellenistic World*. (Studia Orientalia 83.) Helsinki: Finnish Oriental Society.

Karttunen, K. (1999/2000) "King Eucratides in literary sources," *Silk Road Art and Archaeology* 6, 115-118.

Khan, G. M. (1983) "Hathial Excavation," *Journal of Central Asia* 6, 35-44.

Khan, N. A. (1990) "A New Relief from Gandhāra Depicting the Trojan Horse," *East and West* 40, 315-319.

Khozhaniyazov, G. (2006) *The Military Architecture of Ancient Chorasmia (6th century B.C. - 4th century A.D.)*. (Persika 7.) Paris: De Boccard.

Koch, H. (1993) "Feuertempel oder Verwaltungszentrale? Überlegungen zu den Grabungen in Takhte Sangin am Oxos," *Archäologische Mitteilungen aus Iran* 26, 175-186.

Kochelenko, G. (1986) "Les fortifications de l'Orient hellénistique, quelques remarques préliminaires," in Pierre Leriche and Henri Tréziny (eds.), *La fortification dans l'histoire du monde grec : actes du Colloque international La Fortification et sa place dans l'histoire politique, culturelle et sociale du monde grec, Valbonne, décembre 1982*, 143-148. (Colloques internationaux du Centre national de la recherche scientifique 614) Paris: Éditions du Centre national de la Recherche scientifique.

Konow, S. (1929) *Kharoshthi Inscriptions*. (Corpus Inscriptionum Indicarum Vol. 2 Pt. 1.) Calcutta:

Konow, S. (1947) "Note on the Bajaur inscription of Menandros," *Epigraphia Indica* 27, 52-58.

Kopytoff, I. (1986) "The Cultural Biography of Things: Commodotization as Process," in Arjun Appadurai (eds.), *The Social Life of Things: Commodities in Cultural Perspective*, 64-91. Cambridge: Cambridge University Press.

Kordosis, M. (1994) "China and the Greek World: An Introduction to Greek-Chinese Studies with Special Reference to the Chinese Sources," *Historikogeographika* 4, 253-304.

Kosambi, D. D. (1959) "Notes on the Kandahar Edict of Asoka," *Journal of the Economic and Social History of the Orient* 2, 204-206.

Koshelenko, G., V. Gaibov and A. Bader (1996) "Evolution of the Settlement Patterns in the Merv Oasis (Turkmenistan) from Alexander the Great to Arab Conquest," in [...] (eds.), *La Persia e l'Asia Centrale da Alessandro al X secolo*, 305-317. (Atti dei convegni lincei 127.) Rome: Accademia nazionale dei Lincei 127.

Kritt, B. (2001) *Dynastic Transitions in the Coinage of Bactria: Antiochus-Diodotus-Euthydemus*. (Classical Numismatic Studies 4.) Lancaster, PA: Classical Numismatic Group.

Kruglikova, G. I. and V. I. Sarianidi (1971) "Археологические исследования в Северном Афганистане," *Археологические Открытия* 1970, 457-459. ['Archaeological Research in Northern Afghanistan,' *Arkheologicheskie Otkrytiya*.]

Kruglikova, I. T. (1973) "Городище Емши-тепе в северном Афганистане," *Краткие сообщения Института археологии Академии Наук СССР* 136, 104-113. ['The Site of Emshi-tepe in Northern Afghanistan,' *Kratkie sooboshcheniya Instituta arkheologii Akademii Nauk SSSR*.]

Kruglikova, I. T. (1974) *Дильберджин (раскопки 1970 – 1972 гг). Часть 1*. (Материалы к археологической карте Северного Афганистана, выпуск 2.) Moscow: Nauka. [*Dil'berdzhin (Excavations 1970-1972). Part 1*.]

Kruglikova, I. T. (1976a) "Настенные росписи Дильберджина," in I. T. Kruglikova (eds.), *Древняя Бактия: Материалы Советско-Афганской экспедиции 1969-1973 гг*, 87-110. Moscow: Nauka. ['The Wall-Paintings of Dil'berdzhin,' *Drevnyaya Baktriya: Materialy Sovetsko-Afganskoi Ekspeditsii*.]

Kruglikova, I. T. (1977) "Les fouilles de la mission archéologique Soviéto-Afghane sur le site gréco-kushan de Dilberdjin en Bactriane (Afghanistan)," *Comptes-rendus de l'Académie des inscriptions et belles-lettres* 407-427.

Kruglikova, I. T. (1986) *Дильберджин, Храм Диоскуров: Материалы советско-афганской археологической экспедиции*. Moscow: Nauka. [*Dil'berdzhin, Temple of the Dioscuri: Material from the Soviet-Afghan Archaeological Expedition*.]

Kruglikova, I. T. eds. (1976b) *Древняя Бактия: Материалы Советско-Афганской экспедиции 1969-1973 гг*. Moscow: Nauka. [*Ancient Bactria: Material from the Soviet-Afghan Archaeological Expedition/ Drevnyaya Baktriya: Materialy sovetsko-afganskoi arkheologicheskoi ekspeditsii*]

Kruglikova, I. T. and S. Mustamandi (1970) "Résultats préliminaires des travaux de l'Expedition archéologique Afghano-Soviétique en 1969," *Afghanistan* 23, 84-97.

Kruglikova, I. T. and G. A. Pugachenkova (1977) *Дильберджин (раскопки 1970 – 1973 гг). Часть 2*. (Материалы к археологической карте Северного Афганистана, выпуск 3.) Moscow: Nauka.

Kuhrt, A. and S. Sherwin-White eds. (1987) *Hellenism in the East: The interaction of Greek and non-Greek civilizations from Syria to Central Asia after Alexander*. London: Duckworth.

Kurz, O. (1954) "Begram et l'occident gréco-romain," in J. Hackin (eds.), *Nouvelles recherches archéologiques à Begram, Vol. 1*, 93-146. (Mémoires de la Délégation Archéologique Française en Afghanistan 11.) Paris: Imprimerie Nationale-Presses Universitaires.

Kuz'mina, E. E. (1976) "The "Bactrian Mirage" and the Archaeological Reality: On the Problem of the Formation of North Bactrian Culture," *East and West* 26, 111-131.

La Croce, E. (1989) "El papiro de Ai Khanum," *Méthexis* 2, 69-72.

Le Berre, M. and D. Schlumberger (1964) "Observations sur les remparts de Bactres," in Bruno Dagens, Marc Le Berre and Daniel Schlumberger (eds.), *Monuments préislamiques d'Afghanistan*, 61-102. (Mémoires de la Délégation archéologique française en Afghanistan 19.) Paris: Klincksieck.

Lecomte, O. (2007) "Entre Iran et Touran, Recherches archéologiques au Turkménistan méridional (2001-2006)," *Comptes-rendus de l'Académie des inscriptions et belles-lettres* 195-226.

Lecuyot, G. (2005) "Essai de restitution 3D de la ville d'Aï Khanoum en Afghanistan," in Osmund Bopearachchi and Marie-Françoise Boussac (eds.), *Afghanistan: Ancien carrefour entre l'est et l'ouest*, 187-196. (Indicopleustoi: Archaeologies of the Indian Ocean 3.) Turnhout: Brepols.

Lecuyot, G. (2007) "Ai Khanoum Reconstructed," in Joe Cribb and Georgina Herrmann (eds.), *After Alexander: Central Asia Before Islam*, 155-162. (Proceedings of the British Academy 133.) Oxford: Oxford University Press for the British Academy.

Leeming, M. (2003) "Alexander in Afghanistan," *Anglo-Hellenic Review* 27, 12.

Leo, J. (15 March 1999) "Tower of Pomobabble," *U. S. News & World Report*, 16.

Leriche, P. (1974) "Aï Khanoum: un rempart hellénistique en Asie centrale," *Revue Archéologique* 231-270.

Leriche, P. (1985) "Structures politiques et sociales dans la Bactriane et la Sogdiane hellénistiques," in H. Kreissig and F. Kühnert (eds.), *Antike Abhängigkeitsformen in den Griechischen Gebieten ohne Polisstruktur und den Römischen Provinzen, Actes du Colloque sur l'Esclavage, Iéna 29 September – 2 Octobre 1981*, 65-79. (Schriften zur Geschichte und Kultur der Antike 25.) Berlin: Akademie Verlag.

Leriche, P. (1986a) "Fortifications grecques : bilan des recherches récentes au Proche et Moyen Orient," in Pierre Leriche and Henri Tréziny (eds.), *La fortification dans l'histoire du monde grec : actes du Colloque international La Fortification et sa place dans l'histoire politique, culturelle et sociale du monde grec, Valbonne, décembre 1982*, 39-49. (Colloques internationaux du Centre national de la recherche scientifique 614) Paris: Éditions du Centre national de la Recherche scientifique.

Leriche, P. (1986b) *Fouilles d'Aï Khanoum V. Les remparts et les monuments associés*. (Mémoires de la Délégation Archéologique Française en Afghanistan 29.) Paris: De Boccard.

Leriche, P. (2001a) "Bibliographie complémentaire par site du Sourkhan Darya," in P. Leriche, C. Pidaev, M. Gelin, K. Abdoullaev and V. Fourniau (eds.), *La Bactriane au carrefour des routes et des civilisations de l'Asie centrale: Termez et les villes de Bactriane-Tokharestan: Actes du colloque de Termez 1997*, 417-422. (La Bibliothèque d'Asie centrale 1.) Paris: Maisonneuve & Larose; IFEAC.

Leriche, P. (2001b) "Termez antique et médiévale," in P. Leriche, C. Pidaev, M. Gelin, K. Abdoullaev and V. Fourniau (eds.), *La Bactriane au carrefour des routes et des civilisations de l'Asie centrale: Termez et les villes de Bactriane-Tokharestan: Actes du colloque de Termez 1997*, 75-99. (La Bibliothèque d'Asie centrale 1.) Paris: Maisonneuve & Larose; IFEAC.

Leriche, P. (2002) "Termez fondation d'Alexandre?," *Journal Asiatique* 290, 411-415.

Leriche, P. (2007) "Bactria, Land of a Thousand Cities," in Joe Cribb and Georgina Herrmann (eds.), *After Alexander: Central Asia Before Islam*, 121-153. (Proceedings of the British Academy 133.) Oxford: Oxford University Press for the British Academy.

Leriche, P. and T. Annaev (1996) "Bilan des travaux de la MAFOUZ de Bactriane (Mission archéologique franco-ouzbèque de Bctriane septentrionale)," in [...] (eds.), *La Persia e l'Asia Centrale da Alessandro al X secolo*, 277-303. (Atti dei convegni lincei 127.) Rome: Accademia nazionale dei Lincei 127.

Leriche, P. and O. Callot (1986) "Observations sur les remparts de brique crue d'Aï Khanoum et Doura Europos," in Pierre Leriche and Henri Tréziny (eds.), *La fortification dans l'histoire du monde grec : actes du Colloque international La Fortification et sa place dans l'histoire politique, culturelle et sociale du monde grec, Valbonne, décembre 1982*, 289-298. (Colloques internationaux du Centre national de la recherche scientifique 614) Paris: Éditions du Centre national de la Recherche scientifique.

Leriche, P. and C. Pidaev (2008) *Termez sur Oxus. Cité-capitale d Asie Centrale.* (Publication AUROHE 3.) Paris: Maisonneuve & Larose.

Leriche, P., C. Pidaev, M. Gelin, K. Abdoullaev and V. Fourniau eds. (2001) *La Bactriane au carrefour des routes et des civilisations de l'Asie centrale: Termez et les villes de Bactriane-Tokharestan: Actes du colloque de Termez 1997.* (La Bibliothèque d'Asie centrale 1.) Paris: Maisonneuve & Larose; IFEAC.

Leriche, P. and S. Pidaev (2001) "L'action de la Mission Archéologique Franco-Ouzbèque de Bactriane," *Cahiers d'Asie centrale* 9, 243-248.

Leriche, P. and S. Pidaev (2007) "Termez in Antiquity," in Joe Cribb and Georgina Herrmann (eds.), *After Alexander: Central Asia Before Islam*, 179-211. (Proceedings of the British Academy 133.) Oxford: Oxford University Press for the British Academy.

Leriche, P. and J. Thoraval (1979) "La fontaine du rempart de l'Oxus a Aï Khanoum," *Syria* 56, 171-205.

Leriche, P. and H. Tréziny eds. (1986) *La fortification dans l'histoire du monde grec : actes du Colloque international La Fortification et sa place dans l'histoire politique, culturelle et sociale du monde grec, Valbonne, décembre 1982.* (Colloques internationaux du Centre national de la recherche scientifique 614) Paris: Éditions du Centre national de la Recherche scientifique.

Lerner, J. D. (1999) *The Impact of Seleucid Decline on the Eastern Iranian Plateau: The Foundations of Arsacid Parthia and Graeco-Bactria.* (Historia Einzelschriften 123.) Stuttgart: Franz Steiner.

Lerner, J. D. (2003) "The Aï Khanoum Philosophical Papyrus," *Zeitschrift für Papyrologie und Epigraphik* 142, 45-51.

Lerner, J. D. (2003-2004) "Correcting the Early History of Ay Kanom," *Archäologische Mitteilungen aus Iran und Turan* 35-36, 373-410.

Lézire, A. (1964) "Hérat: Notes de Voyage," *Bulletin d'Études Orientales* 18, 127-145.

Liger, J.-C. (1979) *La physionomie urbaine d'une cité hellénistique en Asie Centrale.* Unpublished Maîtrise Thesis. Département d'Urbanisme, Université de Paris VIII.

Litvinskii, B. A. (2001) *Храм Окса в Бактрии (Южный Таджикистан). Том 2: Бактрийское Вооружение в Древневосточном и Греческом Контексте.* Moscow: Vostochnaya Literatura. [*The Temple of the Oxus in Bactria (Southern Tadzhikistan). Vol. 2: Bactrian Arms in the Ancient Eastern and Greek Context.*]

Litvinskii, B. A. and K. Mukhitdinov (1969) "Античное Городище Саксанохур (Южный Таджикистан)," *Советская Археология* 160-178. ['The Ancient Site of Saksanokhur (Southern Tadzhikistan),' *Sovyetskaya Arkheologiya.*]

Litvinskii, B. A. and I. R. Pichikian (1994) "The Hellenistic Architecture and Art of the Temple of the Oxus," *Bulletin of the Asia Institute, New Series* 8 (Studies from the Former Soviet Union) 47-66.

Litvinskii, B. A. and I. R. Pichikyan (2000) *Эллинистический Храм Окса в Бактрии (Южный Таджикистан). Том 1: Раскопки, Архитектура, Религиозная Жизнь.* Moscow: Vostochnaya Literatura. [*The Hellenistic Temple of the Oxus in Bactria (Southern Tadzhikistan). Vol. 1: Excavations, Architecture, Religious Life.*]

Litvinskii, B. A. and A. V. Sedov (1984) *Культы и Ритуалы Кушанской Бактрии: Погребалный Обряд.* Moscow: Nauka. [*Cults and Rituals of Kushan Bactria: Funerary Ritual.*]

Litvinskii, B. A. and V. S. Solokov'ev (1985) *Средневековая культура Тохаристана в свете раскопок в Вахшской долине.* (Академия Наук СССР ордена трудного красного знамени институт востоковедения; Академия Наук Таджикской ССР институт истории им. А. Долиша.) Moscow: Nauka. [*The Material Culture of Tokharistan, in the Light of Excavations in the Vakhsh Valley.*]

Litvinskii, B. A., Y. G. Vinogradov and I. R. Pichikyan (1985) "Вотив Атросока из Храма Окса в Северной Бактрии," *Вестник Древней Истории* 85-110. ['The Votive Offering of Atrosokes, From the Temple of the Oxus in Northern Bactria,' *Вестник Древнеи Истории.*]

Litvinskii, B. A. and T. I. Zeimal' (1971) *Аджина-Тепе. Архитектура, скульптура, живопись.* Moscow: Iskusstvo. [*Adzhina-tepe. Architecture, Sculpture, Painting.*]

Litvinskij, B. A. (1985) "Problèmes d'histoire et d'histoire culturelle de la Bactriane à la lumière des fouilles menées dans le Tadjikistan méridional," in M. S. et al. Asimov (eds.),

Litvinskij, B. A. and I. R. Pičikian (1995a) "An Achaemenian griffin-handle from the temple of the Oxus. The makhaira in northern Bactria," in A. Invernizzi (eds.), *In the Land of the Gryphons: Papers on Central Asian Archaeology in Antiquity*, 107-128. (Monografie di Mesopotamia 5.) Firenze: Casa Editrice Le Lettere.

Litvinskij, B. A. and I. R. Pičikian (1995b) "River-Deities of Greece Salute the God of the River Oxus-Vaksh: Achelous and the Hippocampess," in A. Invernizzi (eds.), *In the Land of the Gryphons: Papers on Central Asian Archaeology in Antiquity*, 129-149. (Monografie di Mesopotamia 5.) Firenze: Casa Editrice Le Lettere.

Litvinskij, B. A. and I. R. Pičikjan (2002) *Taxt-i Sangin, der Oxus-Tempel: Grabungsbefund, Statigraphie und Architektur*. (Archäologie in Iran und Turan 4.) Mainz am Rhein: Philip von Zabern.

Litvinskij, B. A. and T. I. Zejmal' (2004) *The Buddhist Monastery of Ajina Tepa, Tajikistan: History and Art of Buddhism in Central Asia*. (Istituto Italiano per l'Africa e l'Oriente, Centro scavi e richerche archeologiche; Academy of Sciences of Tajikistan; Reports an Memoirs, New Series, Volume 1.) Rome: Istituto Italiano per l'Africa e l'Oriente.

Litvinskiy, B. A. and I. R. Pichikiyan (1981) "The Temple of the Oxus," *Journal of the Royal Asiatic Society* 133-167.

Litvinskiy, B. A. and I. R. Pichikyan (1984) "Monuments of Art from the Sanctuary of the Oxus (Northern Bactria)," in J. Harmatta (eds.), *From Hecataeus to Al-Ḫuwārizmī, Bactrian, Pahlavi, Sogidan, Persian, Sanskrit, Syriac, Arabic, Chinese, Greek and Latin Sources for the History of Pre-Islamic Central Asia*, 25-83. (Collection of the Sources for the History of Pre-Islamic Central Asia 1.3.) Budapest: Akadémiaí Kiadó.

Litvinsky, B. A. and I. R. Pichikian (1998) "The Ionic Capital from the Temple of the Oxus (Northern Bactria)," *Iranica Antiqua* 33, 233-258.

Litvinsky, B. A. and I. R. Pichikjan (1995) "Gold Plaques from the Oxus Temple (Northern Bactria)," *Ancient Civilizations from Scythia to Siberia* 2, 196-220.

Litvinsky, B. A. and I. R. Pichikyan (2002) "Three Major Discoveries in Bactria," in Miho Museum (eds.), *Treasures of Ancient Bactria*, 213-219. Shigaraki: Miho Museum.

Lo Muzio, C. (1999) "The Dioscuri at Dilberjin (Northern Afghanistan): Reviewing their Chronology and Significance," *Studia Iranica* 28, 41-71.

Lundbæk, K. (1986) *T.S. Bayer, 1694-1738: Pioneer Sinologist*. (Scandinavian Institute of Asian Studies Monograph Series 54.) London: Curzon Press.

Lyonnet, B. (1977) "Découverte de sites de l'age du bronze dans le N.E. de l'Afghanistan: leurs rapports avec la civilisation de l'Indus," *Annali dell'Istituto Orientale di Napoli* 37, 19-35.

Lyonnet, B. (1981) "Établissements chalcolithiques dans le Nord-Est de l'Afghanistan: leurs rapports avec les cultures du Bassin de l'Indus," *Paléorient* 7, 57-74.

Lyonnet, B. (1985) "Contributions récentes de la céramologie à l'histoire de l'Afghanistan," *Arts Asiatiques* 40, 41-52.

Lyonnet, B. (1990) "Les rapports entre l'Asie centrale et l'Empire achéménide d'après les données de l'archéologie," *Achaemenid History* 4, 77-92.

Lyonnet, B. (1993) "The Problem of the Frontiers between Bactria and Sogdiana. An Old Discussion and New Data," in A. J. Gail and G. J. R. Mevissen (eds.), *South Asian Archaeology 1991*, 195-208. Berlin:

Lyonnet, B. (1994) "L'occupation séleucide en Bactriane orientale et en Syrie du N.E. d'après les données archéologiques (prospections surtout)," *Topoi* 4, 541-546.

Lyonnet, B. (1997) *Prospections archéologiques en Bactriane orientale (1974-1978). Vol. 2: Céramique et Peuplement du Chalcolithique à la Conquête Arabe*. (Mémoires de la Mission archéologique française en Asie centrale.) Paris: Éditions Recherche sur les Civilisations.

Lyonnet, B. (1998) "Les Grecs, les nomades et l'indépendance de la Sogdiane, d'après l'occupation comparée d'Aï Khanoum et de Marakanda au cours des derniers siècles avant notre ère," *Bulletin of the Asia Institute* 12, 141-159.

Lyonnet, B. (2010) "D'Aï Khanoum à Koktepe. Questions sur la datation absolue de la céramique hellénistique d'Asie centrale," in Kazim Abdullaev (eds.), Традиции Востока и Запада в Античной Культуре Средней Азии:

Сборник Статей в Честь Поля Бернара - The Traditions of East and West in the Antique Cultures of Central Asia: Papers in Honor of Paul Bernard, 141-153. (Институт Археологии Имени Я. Гулямова Академии Наук Республикии Узбекистан - Institute of Archaeology, Academy of Sciences of the Republic of Uzbekistan.) Tashkent: Noshirlik yog'dusi.

Magee, P., C. A. Petrie, J. R. Knox, F. Khan and K. D. Thomas (2005) "The Achaemenid Empire in South Asia and Recent Excavations at Akra in Northwest Pakistan," *American Journal of Archaeology* 109, 711-741.

Mairs, R. (2006a) *Ethnic Identity in the Hellenistic Far East*. Unpublished PhD Thesis. Faculty of Classics, University of Cambridge.

Mairs, R. (2006b) "'Hellenistic India'," *New Voices in Classical Reception* 1, 19-30.

Mairs, R. (2007a) "Egyptian Artefacts from Central and South Asia," in Rachel Mairs and Alice Stevenson (eds.), *Current Research in Egyptology VI*, 74-89. Oxford: Oxbow.

Mairs, R. (2007b) "Ethnicity and Funerary Practice in Hellenistic Bactria," in H. Schroeder, P. Bray, P. Gardner, V. Jefferson and E. Macaulay-Lewis (eds.), *Crossing Frontiers: The opportunities and challenges of interdisciplinary approaches to archaeology*, 111-124. (Oxford University School of Archaeology Monographs 63.) Oxford: School of Archaeology.

Mairs, R. (2008) "Greek Identity and the Settler Community in Hellenistic Bactria and Arachosia," *Migrations and Identities* 1, 19-43.

Mairs, R. (2010a) ""Identity and the Archaeological Record in Hellenistic Bactria" In Jennifer E. Gates-Foster, Beyond Identity in the Hellenistic East," in M. Dalla Riva (eds.), *Meetings between Cultures in the Ancient Mediterranean. Proceedings of the 17th International Congress of Classical Archaeology, Rome 22-26 sept. 2008*, Rome:

Mairs, R. (2010b) "The Places in Between: Model and Metaphor in the Archaeology of Hellenistic Arachosia," in Sujatha Chandrasekaran, Anna Kouremenos and Roberto Rossi (eds.), *From Pella to Gandhara: Hybridisation and Identity in the Art and Architecture of the Hellenistic East*, Oxford: BAR.

Mairs, R. (forthcoming-a) "Administering Bactria: From Achaemenid Satrapy to Graeco-Bactrian State," in Anna Lucille Boozer and Laurence Coben (eds.), *Excavating Empires*, Los Angeles: UCLA Press.

Mairs, R. (forthcoming-b) "The 'Temple with Indented Niches' at Ai Khanoum: Ethnic and Civic Identity in Hellenistic Bactria," in Richard Alston, Onno M. van Nijf and Christina Williamson (eds.), *Cults, Creeds and Contests: Religion in the Post-Classical City*, (Groningen-Royal Hollway Studies on the Greek City after the Classical Age. Volume 3.) Leuven: Peeters.

Majumdar, N. G. (1937) "The Bajaur Casket of the Reign of Menander," *Epigraphia Indica* 24, 1-8.

Malkin, I. (1998) *The Returns of Odysseus: Colonization and Ethnicity*. Berkeley: University of California Press.

Malkin, I. eds. (2001) *Ancient Perceptions of Greek Ethnicity*. (Center for Hellenic Studies Colloquia 5.) Washington, D.C.: Center for Hellenic Studies; Trustees for Harvard University.

Mandel'shtam, A. M. and S. B. Pevzner (1958) "Работы Кафирниганского отряда в 1952-1953 гг.," *Материалы и исследования по археологии СССР* 66, 290-324.

Marshall, J. H. (1951) *Taxila: An Illustrated Account*. Cambridge: Cambridge University Press.

Marshall, J. H. (1960) *A Guide to Taxila*. Cambridge: Cambridge University Press.

Masson, V. M. (1966) *Страна тысячи городов*. (Академия Наук СССР.) Moscow: Nauka.

Masson, V. M. (1982) *Das Land der tausend Städte: Die Wiederentdeckung der ältesten Kulturgebiete in Mittelasien*. München: Udo Pfriemer.

McNicoll, A. (1978) "Excavations at Kandahar, 1975: Second Interim Report," *Afghan Studies* 1, 41-66.

McNicoll, A. and W. Ball (1996) *Excavations at Kandahar 1974 and 1975: The First Two Seasons at Shahr-i Kohna (Old Kandahar) Conducted by the British Institute of Afghan Studies*. (BAR International Series 641; Society for South Asian Studies Monograph 1.) Oxford: BAR Publishing.

Mehendale, S. (1997) *Begram: New Perspectives on the Ivory and Bone Carvings [Online with database at http://ecai.org/begramweb/]*. Unpublished Thesis. University of California.

Mehendale, S. (2001) "The Begram Ivory and Bone Carvings : some Observations on Provenance and Chronology," *Topoi Orient-Occident* 11, 485-514.

Menninger, M. (1996) *Untersuchungen zu den Gläsern und Gipsabgüssen aus dem Fund von Begram (Afghanistan)*. (Würzburger Forschungen zur Altertumskunde 1.) Würzburg: ERGON.

Miho Museum (2002) *Treasures of Ancient Bactria. Catalog of an exhibition held at the Miho Museum, Aug. 18 -Sept. 1 2002*. Shigaraki: Miho Museum.

Mitchell, S. and G. Greatrex eds. (2000) *Ethnicity and Culture in Late Antiquity*. London: Duckworth; The Classical Press of Wales.

Mongait, A. L. (1961) *Archaeology in the U.S.S.R.* Harmondsworth: Penguin.

Mukherjee, B. N. (1984) *Studies in Aramaic Edicts of Aśoka*. Calcutta: Indian Museum.

Mukherjee, B. N. (1986) "The Problem of Attribution of the Reh Inscription," *Information Bulletin, International Association for the Study for the Cultures of Central Asia* 11, 43-48.

Mukhitdinov, K. (1968) "Гончарный квартал городища Саксанохур," *Известия Академии Наук Таджикской ССР. Серия общественных наук* 3, ['The Potters' Quarter at the Site of Saksanokhur,' *Izvestiya Akademii Nauk Tadzhikskoi SSR*.]

Narain, A. K. (1957) *The Indo-Greeks*. Oxford: Clarendon Press.

Narain, A. K. (1986) "The Greek Monogram (X) and Aï Khanoum - The Bactrian City," *Numismatic Digest* 10, 4-15.

Narain, A. K. (1987) "Notes on Some Inscriptions from Aï Khanum (Afghanistan)," *Zeitschrift für Papyrologie und Epigraphik* 69, 277-282.

Narain, A. K. (1992) "Approaches and Perspectives," *Yavanika* 2, 5-34.

Naveh, J. and S. Shaked (forthcoming) *Ancient Aramaic Documents from Bactria: 4th Century B.C.E.* (Studies in the Khalili Collection.) Oxford: Khalili Collection.

Negmatov, N. N. (1986) "Archaic Khojent - Alexandria Eschata (To the Problem of Syr-Darya Basin Urbanization)," *Journal of Central Asia* 9, 41-54.

Negmatov, N. N. (1986) *Исследования по истории и культуре Ленинабада*. (Академия Наук Таджикской ССР. Институт Истории им. А. Дониша.) Dushanbe:

Nehru, L. (1999/2000) "Khalchayan Revisited," *Silk Road Art and Archaeology* 6, 217-239.

Neva, E. (2008) *Искусство древних ювелиров (Центральная Азия: IV до н.э. — IV в.)*. [*The Art of Ancient Jewellery (Central Asia: 4th Century BC - 4th Century AD)*.]

Nikonorov, V. P. and S. A. Savchuk (1992) "New Data on Ancient Bactrian Body-Armour (In the Light of Finds from Kampyr Tepe)," *Iran* 30, 49-54.

Norman, K. R. (1972) "Notes on the Greek Version of Aśoka's Twelfth and Thirteenth Rock Edicts," *Journal of the Royal Asiatic Society* 111-118.

Oikonomides, A. N. (1980) "The τέμενος of Alexander the Great at Alexandria in Arachosia (Old Kandahar)," *Zeitschrift für Papyrologie und Epigraphik* 56, 145-147.

Olivier-Utard, F. (1997) *Politique et archéologie: Histoire de la Délégation archéologique française en Afghanistan (1922-1982)*. Paris: Éditions Recherche sur les Civilisations.

Padwa, M. (2004) "Evolving the Archaeological Mapping of Afghanistan," *The Silk Road Newsletter* 2, Retrieved September 24 2010 from <http://www.silk-road.com/newsletter/vol2012num2012/Evolving.html>.

Parasher, A. (1991) *Mlecchas in Early India: A Study in Attitudes Towards Outsiders up to AD 600*. New Delhi: Munshiram Manoharlal.

Parnicki, T. (1991) *La Fin de «L'Entente des peuples»*. Montricher: Les Éditions Noir sur Blanc

Penny Cyclopædia (1835) "Bactria, or Bactriana (now Bokhara)," in [...] (eds.), *The Penny Cyclopædia of the Society for the Diffusion of Useful Knowledge. Volume III: Athanaric-Bassano*, 252-254. London: Charles Knight.

Pestman, P. W. (1981) *A Guide to the Zenon Archive (P. L. Bat. 21)*. (Papyrologica Lugduno-Batava 21.) Leiden: E. J. Brill.

Petrie, C. A. and P. Magee (2007) "Histories, epigraphy and authority: Achaemenid and indigenous control in Pakistan in the 1st millennium BC," *Gandharan Studies* 1,

Petrie, C. A., P. Magee and M. N. Khan (2008) "Emulation at the edge of empire: the adoption of non-local vessels forms in the NWFP,

Pakistan during the mid-late 1st millennium BC," *Gandharan Studies* 2, 1-16.

Pfrommer, M. (1993) *Metalwork from the Hellenized East: Catalogue of the Collections*. Malibu: J. Paul Getty Museum.

Picard, O. (1984) "Sur deux termes des inscriptions de la trésorerie d'Aï Khanoum," in Hélène Walter (eds.), *Hommages à Lucien Lerat. Vol. II.*, 679-690. (Annales littéraires de l'Université de Besançon 294; Centre de recherches d'histoire ancienne 55.) Paris: Les Belles lettres.

Pichikian, I. R. (1991) Культура Бактрии: ахеменидский и эллинистический периоду. Moscow: Nauka. [*The Culture of Bactria: Achaemenid and Hellenistic Period.*]

Pichikjan, I. R. (1985) "Les composantes de la culture gréco-bactrienne (d'après les matériaux du Temple de l'Oxus a Takhti Sangin)," in M. S. et al. Asimov (eds.), *L'archéologie de la Bactriane ancienne. Actes du Colloque franco-soviétique, Dushanbe (U.R.S.S.), 27 octobre – 3 novembre 1982*, 281-283. Paris: CNRS.

Pichikyan, I. R. (1987a) "The Graeco-Bactrian Altars in the Temple of the Oxus," *Information Bulletin, International Association for the Study for the Cultures of Central Asia* 12, 56-65.

Pichikyan, I. R. (1987b) "The Oxus Temple Composition in the Context of Architectural Comparison," *Information Bulletin, International Association for the Study for the Cultures of Central Asia* 12, 42-56.

Pichikyan, I. R. (1989) "Открытие теменоса храма Окса (Северная Бактрия)," Вестник Древней Истории 1989/4, 113-116. [The Discovery of the Temenos of the Temple of the Oxus (Northern Bactria).]

Pichikyan, I. R. (1997) "Rebirth of the Oxus Treasure: Second Part of the Oxus Treasure from the Miho Museum Collection," *Ancient Civilizations from Scythia to Siberia* 4, 306-383.

Pichikyan, I. R. (1998a) "Возрождение большого клада Окса. Вторая часть клада Окса из коллекции Михо Музея II," Вестник Древней Истории 2(225), 161-186. ['The Rebirth of the Great Hoard of the Oxus. The Second Part of the Oxus Treasure, from the Collection of the Miho Museum II,' *Vestnik Drevnei Istorii*.]

Pichikyan, I. R. (1998b) "Возрождение большого клада Окса. Вторая часть клада Окса из коллекции Михо Музея I," Вестник Древней Истории 1(224), 92-107. ['The Rebirth of the Great Hoard of the Oxus. The Second Part of the Oxus Treasure, from the Collection of the Miho Museum I,' *Vestnik Drevnei Istorii*.]

Pidaev, S. R. (1974) "Материалы к изучению древних памятников Северной Бактрии," in V. M. Masson (eds.), Древняя Бактрия: предварительные сообщения об археологических работах на юге Узбекистана, 32-41. Leningrad: Nauka. ['Materials for the Study of Ancient Monuments in Northern Bactria,' *Drevnyaya Baktriya: predvaritel'nye soobshcheniya ob arkheologicheskikh rabotakh na yuge Uzbekistana*.]

Pidaev, S. R. (1984) "Керамика Джига-тепе (из раскопок 1976 г.)," in I. T. Kruglikova (eds.), Древняя Бактия 3: Материалы советско-афганской археологической экспедиции, 112-124. Moscow: Nauka. ['Ceramics of Dzhiga-tepe (from the 1976 Excavations),' *Drevnyaya Baktriya 3: Materialy sovetsko-afganskoi arkheologicheskoi ekspeditsii*.]

Pidaev, S. R. (2003) "Termez During the Greco-Bactrian Period," *Silk Road Art and Archaeology* 9, 1-14.

Pilipko, V. (2001) "Les établissements urbains de la Bactriane du nord-ouest," in P. Leriche, C. Pidaev, M. Gelin, K. Abdoullaev and V. Fourniau (eds.), *La Bactriane au carrefour des routes et des civilisations de l'Asie centrale: Termez et les villes de Bactriane-Tokharestan: Actes du colloque de Termez 1997*, 215-218. (La Bibliothèque d'Asie centrale 1.) Paris: Maisonneuve & Larose.

Pirazzoli-t'Serstevens, M. (2001) "Les laques chinois de Begram. Un réexamen de leur identification et de leur datation," *Topoi Orient-Occident* 11, 473-484.

Pitschikjan, I. R. (1992) *Oxos-Schatz und Oxus-Tempel: Achämenidische Kunst in Mittelasien*. (Antike in der Moderne 1.) Berlin: Akademie Verlag.

Posch, W. (1995) *Baktrien zwischen Griechen und Kuschan : Untersuchungen zu kulturellen und historischen Problemen einer Übergangsphase : mit einem textkritischen Exkurs zum Shiji 123*. Wiesbaden: Harrassowitz.

Pougatchenkova, G. A. (1978) *Les trésors de Dalverzine-Tépé*. Leningrad: Éditions d'Art Aurore.

Pougatchenkova, G. A. (1986) "Caractères de l'architecture défensive antique en Asie Centrale," in Pierre Leriche and Henri Tréziny (eds.), *La fortification dans l'histoire du monde grec : actes du Colloque international La Fortification et sa place dans l'histoire politique, culturelle et sociale du monde grec, Valbonne,* décembre 1982, 51-69. (Colloques internationaux du Centre national de la recherche scientifique 614) Paris: Éditions du Centre national de la Recherche scientifique.

Pougatchenkova, G. A. (2001a) "C'était hier ; c'était il y a longtemps (Souvenirs d'une participante à l'éxpedition archéologique de Termez en 1938)," in P. Leriche, C. Pidaev, M. Gelin, K. Abdoullaev and V. Fourniau (eds.), *La Bactriane au carrefour des routes et des civilisations de l'Asie centrale: Termez et les villes de Bactriane-Tokharestan: Actes du colloque de Termez 1997*, 37-46. (La Bibliothèque d'Asie centrale 1.) Paris: Maisonneuve & Larose.

Pougatchenkova, G. A. (2001b) "Histoire des recherches archéologiques en Bactriane septentrionale: Région du Sourkhan Darya, Ouzbékistan (jusqu'à la création de la MAFOuz B)," in P. Leriche, C. Pidaev, M. Gelin, K. Abdoullaev and V. Fourniau (eds.), *La Bactriane au carrefour des routes et des civilisations de l'Asie centrale: Termez et les villes de Bactriane-Tokharestan: Actes du colloque de Termez 1997*, 23-34. (La Bibliothèque d'Asie centrale 1.) Paris: Maisonneuve & Larose.

Pugachenkova, G. A. (1965) "La sculpture de Khaltchayan," *Iranica Antiqua* 5, 116-127.

Pugachenkova, G. A. (1966) Халчаян. К проблеме художественной культуры Северной Бактрии. Tashkent: [*Khalchayan. The Problem of the Artistic Culture of Northern Bactria.*]

Pugachenkova, G. A. (1971) Скульптура Халчаяна. Moscow: Iskusstvo. [*The Sculpture of Khalchayan.*]

Pugachenkova, G. A. (1979) "Жига-тепе (раскопки 1974 г.)," in I. T. Kruglikova (eds.), Древняя Бактия 2: Материалы Советско-Афганской археологической экспедиции, 63-94. Moscow: Nauka. ['Zhiga-tepe (Excavations 1974),' *Drevnyaya Baktriya 2: Materialy sovetsko-afganskoi arkheologicheskoi ekspeditsii.*]

Pugachenkova, G. A. (1984) "Раскопки южных городских ворот Дильберджина," in I. T. Kruglikova (eds.), Древняя Бактия 3: Материалы советско-афганской археологической экспедиции, 93-111. Moscow: Nauka. ['Excavations of the Southern Gate of the City of Dil'berdzhin,' *Drevnyaya Baktriya 3: Materialy sovetsko-afganskoi arkheologicheskoi ekspeditsii.*]

Pugachenkova, G. A. (1987) "Шортепе," История материальнои культуры Узбекистана 21, 21-45. ['Shor-tepe,' *Istoriya material'noi kul'tury Uzbekistana.*]

Pugachenkova, G. A. and E. V. Rtveladze (1978) Дальверзинтепе - Кушанскии город на юге Узбекистана. Taskent: [*Dal'verzin-tepe - A Kushan Town in Southern Uzbekistan.*]

Pugachenkova, G. A. and E. V. Rtveladze (1990) Северная Бактрия-Тохаристан. Очерки истории и культуры: древность и средневековье. (Академия Наук Узбекской ССР: Институт Истории.) Tashkent: Izadel'stvo «Fan». [*Northern Bactria-Tokharistan. Essays on History and Culture: Ancient and Mediaeval.*]

Pugliese Carratelli, G. (1966) "Greek Inscriptions of the Middle East," *East and West* 16, 31-36.

Pugliese Carratelli, G. and G. Garbini (1964) *A Bilingual Graeco-Aramaic Edict by Asoka. The First Greek Inscription Discovered in Afghanistan.* (Serie Orientale Roma 29.) Rome: Istituto italiano per il medio ed estremo Oriente.

Pugliese Carratelli, G., G. Levi Della Vida, G. Tucci and U. Scerrato (1958) *Un editto bilingue greco-aramaico di Asoka. La prima inscrizione greca scoperta in Afghanistan.* Rome: Istituto italiano per il medio ed estremo Oriente.

Rapin, C. (1983) "Les inscriptions économiques de la trésorerie hellénistique d'Aï Khanoum (Afghanistan)," *Bulletin de Correspondance Hellénique* 107, 315-381.

Rapin, C. (1987) "La trésorerie hellénistique d'Aï Khanoum," *Revue Archéologique* 41-70.

Rapin, C. (1990) "Greeks in Afghanistan: Aï Khanum," in J.-P. Descœudres (eds.), *Greek Colonists and Native Populations, Proceedings of the First Australian Congress of Classical Archaeology Held in Honour of Emeritus Professor A. D. Trendall*, 329-342. Canberra; Oxford: Humanities Research Centre; Clarendon Press.

Rapin, C. (1992) *Fouilles d'Aï Khanoum VIII: La trésorerie du palais hellénistique d'Aï Khanoum, l'apogée et la chute du royaume grec de Bactriane.* (Mémoires de la Délégation Archéologique Française en Afghanistan 33.) Paris: de Boccard.

Rapin, C. (1995) "Hinduism in the Indo-Greek Area: Notes on Some Indian Finds from Bactria and on Two Temples in Taxila," in A. Invernizzi (eds.), *In the Land of the Gryphons: Papers on Central Asian Archaeology in Antiquity*, 275-291. (Monografie di Mesopotamia 5.) Firenze: Casa Editrice Le Lettere.

Rapin, C. (1996a) *Indian Art from Afghanistan: The legend of Śakuntalā and the Indian Treasure of Eucratides at Ai Khanum*. New Delhi: Manohar.

Rapin, C. (1996b) "Nouvelles observations sur le parchemin gréco-bactrien d'Asangôrna," *Topoi* 6, 458-469.

Rapin, C. (1998) "L'incompréhensible Asie centrale de la carte de Ptolémée. Propositions pour un décodage," *Bulletin of the Asia Institute* 12, 201-225.

Rapin, C. (2003) "Le nom antique d'Aï Khanoum et de son fleuve," in Osmund Bopearachchi, Christian Landes and Christine Sachs (eds.), *De l'Indus à l'Oxus: Archéologie de l'Asie centrale. Catalogue de l'exposition*, 115. Lattes: Association imago-musée de Lattes.

Rapin, C. (2003) "Les Portes de Fer de Derbent: histoire d'une frontière," *Au fil des routes de la soie, Chemins d'étoiles, invitations à l'itinérance* 11, 148-156.

Rapin, C. (2005) "L'Afghanistan et l'Asie centrale dans la géographie mythique des historiens d'Alexandre et dans la toponymie des géographes gréco-romains. Notes sur la route d'Herat à Begram," in Osmund Bopearachchi and Marie-Françoise Boussac (eds.), *Afghanistan: Ancien carrefour entre l'est et l'ouest*, 143-172. (Indicopleustoi: Archaeologies of the Indian Ocean 3.) Turnhout: Brepols.

Rapin, C. (2007) "Nomads and the Shaping of Central Asia: From the Early Iron Age to the Kushan Period," in Joe Cribb and Georgina Herrmann (eds.), *After Alexander: Central Asia Before Islam*, 29-72. (Proceedings of the British Academy 133.) Oxford: Oxford University Press for the British Academy.

Rapin, C. (2010) "L'ère Yavana d'après les parchemins gréco-bactriens d'Asangorna et d'Amphipolis," in Kazim Abdullaev (eds.), *Традиции Востока и Запада в Античной Культуре Средней Азии: Сборник Статей в Честь Поля Бернара - The Traditions of East and West in the Antique Cultures of Central Asia: Papers in Honor of Paul Bernard*, 234-252. (Институт Археологии Имени Я. Гулямова Академии Наук Республикии Узбекистан - Institute of Archaeology, Academy of Sciences of the Republic of Uzbekistan.) Tashkent: Noshirlik yog'dusi.

Rapin, C., A. Baud, F. Grenet and S. A. Rakhmanov (2006) "Les recherches sur la region des Portes de Fer de Sogdiane: bref état des questions en 2005," *История материальнои культуры Узбекистана* 35, 91-112. [*Istoriya material'noi kul'tury Uzbekistana.*]

Rapin, C. and P. Hadot (1987) "Les textes littéraires grecs de la trésorerie d'Aï Khanoum," *Bulletin de Correspondance Hellénique* 111, 225-266.

Rapin, C. and M. Isamiddinov (1994) "Fortifications hellénistiques de Samarcande (Samarkand-Afrasiab)," *Topoi* 4, 547-565.

Rapin, C., M. Isamiddinov and M. Khasanov (2001) "La tombe d'une princesse nomade à Koktepe près de Samarkand," *Comptes-rendus de l'Académie des inscriptions et belles-lettres* 145, 33-92.

Rapin, C. and S. A. Rakhmanov (1999) "Les 'Portes de Fer' près de Derbent," *Dossiers d'Archéologie* 243, 18-19.

Rawlinson, H. G. (1909) *Bactria: From the Earliest Times to the Extinction of Bactrio-Greek Rule in the Punjab (being the Hare University Prize Essay, 1908)*. Bombay: The 'Times of India' Office.

Ray, H. P. (1988) "The Yavana Presence in Ancient India," *Journal of the Economic and Social History of the Orient* 31, 311-325.

Rea, J., R. C. Senior and A. S. Hollis (1994) "A Tax Receipt from Hellenstic Bactria," *Zeitschrift für Papyrologie und Epigraphik* 104, 261-280.

Reiss-Engelhorn-Museen (2009) *Alexander der Grosse und die Öffnung der Welt : Asiens Kulturen im Wandel*. (Publikationen der Reiss-Engelhorn-Museen 36.) Regensburg: Schnell & Steiner GmbH.

Rhys-Davids, T. W. (1890) *The Questions of King Milinda*. (Sacred Books of the East 35 and 36.) Oxford: Oxford University Press.

Robert, L. (1968) "De Delphes à l'Oxus: Inscriptions grecques nouvelles de la Bactriane," *Comptes-rendus de l'Académie des inscriptions et belles-lettres* 416-457.

Robert, L. (1973) "Les inscriptions," in Paul Bernard (eds.), *Fouilles d'Aï Khanoum I (Campagnes 1965, 1966, 1967, 1968), Vol. 1*, 207-237. (Mémoires de la Délégation archéologique française en Afghanistan 21.) Paris: Klincksieck.

Rondelli, B. and S. Mantellini (2004) "Methods and Perspectives for Ancient Settlement Studies in the Middle Zeravshan Valley," *The Silk Road Newsletter* 2, Retrieved September 24 2010 from <http://www.silk-road.com/newsletter/vol2012num2012/Zeravshan.html>.

Rougemont, G. (2005) "Nouvelles inscriptions grecques de l'Asie Centrale," in Osmund Bopearachchi and Marie-Françoise Boussac (eds.), *Afghanistan: Ancien carrefour entre l'est et l'ouest*, 127-136. (Indicopleustoi: Archaeologies of the Indian Ocean 3.) Turnhout: Brepols.

Rowland, B. (1966) *Ancient Art from Afghanistan: Treasures of the Kabul Museum. (Asia House Gallery, New York City: January 13 - March 6, 1966; The Los Angeles County Museum of Art, Lytton Gallery: March 25 - May 16, 1966; National Collection of Fine Arts, Smithsonian Institution, Washington D.C.: June 29 - August 23, 1966.)*. New York: The Asia Society.

Rowland, B. (1971) *Art in Afghanistan: Objects from the Kabul Museum*. London: Allen Lane, The Penguin Press.

Royal Academy of Arts ([1967]) *Ancient Art from Afghanistan, at the Royal Academy of Arts, 6 December 1967 to 28 January 1968*. London: The Arts Council.

Rtveladze, E. V. (1977) "Несколько Древнеегипетских Предметов из Северной Бактрии," *Советская Археология* 1977/2, 235-238. ['Some Ancient Egyptian Objects from Northern Bactria,' *Sovetskaya Arkheologiya*.]

Rtveladze, E. V. (1984a) "La circulation monétaire au Nord de l'Oxus à l'époque gréco-bactrienne," *Revue Numismatique* 6, 61-76.

Rtveladze, E. V. (1984b) "Кушанская крепость Кампыр-тепе (Исследования и открытия)," *Вестник Древней Истории* 1984, 87-106. ['The Kushan Fort of Kampyr-tepe,' *Vestnik Drvnei Istorii*.]

Rtveladze, E. V. (1990) "Из недавних открытий узбекистанской искусствоведческой експедиции в северной Бактрии-Тохаристане," *Вестник Древней Истории* 145-147. ['Recent Discoveries of the Uzbek Art-Historical Expedition in Northern Bactria-Tokharistan,' *Vestnik drevnei Istorii*.]

Rtveladze, E. V. (1994) "Kampir-Tepe: Structures, Written Documents, and Coins," in B. A. Litvinskii and C. Altman-Bromberg (eds.), *The Archaeology and Art of Central Asia: Studies from the Former Soviet Union*, 141-154. (Bulletin of the Asia Institute NS 8.) Bloomfield, MI:

Rtveladze, E. V. (1995) "Découvertes en numismatique et épigraphie gréco-bactriennes à Kampyr-Tepe (Bactriane du nord)," *Revue Numismatique* 6, 20-24.

Rtveladze, E. V. (1999) "Kampyr Tepe-Pandokheïon," *Dossiers d'Archéologie* 247, 56-57.

Rtveladze, E. V. eds. (2000) *Материалы Тохаристанской экспедиции. Археологические исследования Кампыртепа [I]*. Tashkent: San'at. [*Material from the Tokharistan Expedition. Archaeological Study of Kampyr-tepe [I]*]

Rtveladze, E. V. eds. (2001) *Материалы Тохаристанской экспедиции. Археологические исследования Кампыртепа II*. Tashkent: San'at. [*Material from the Tokharistan Expedition. Archaeological Study of Kampyr-tepe (II)*]

Rtveladze, E. V. eds. (2002) *Материалы Тохаристанской экспедиции. Археологические исследования Кампыртепа III*. Tashkent: San'at. [Material from the Tokharistan Expedition. Archaeological Study of Kampyr-tepe (III)]

Rtveladze, E. V. eds. (2006) *Материалы Тохаристанской экспедиции. Археологические исследования Кампыртепа и Шортепа V*. Tashkent: San'at. [*Material from the Tokharistan Expedition. Archaeological Study of Kampyr-tepe and Shor-tepe (V)*]

Rtveladze, E. V. and A. S. Sagdullaev (1985) "Les particularités du peuplement du Surkhandar'ja à l'Age du Bronze et au début de l'Age du Fer," in M. S. et al. Asimov (eds.), *L'archéologie de la Bactriane ancienne. Actes du Colloque franco-soviétique, Dushanbe (U.R.S.S.), 27 octobre – 3 novembre 1982*, 187-193. Paris: CNRS.

Rtweladse, E. V. (2009) "Kampyr-Tepe-Pandocheion - Alexandria Oxiana," in Reiss Engelhorn Museen (eds.), *Alexander der Grosse und die Öffnung der Welt : Asiens Kulturen im Wandel*, 169-175. (Publikationen der Reiss-Engelhorn-Museen 36.) Regensburg: Schnell & Steiner GmbH.

Rusanov, D. V. (1994) "The Fortifications of Kampir-Tepe: A Reconstruction," in B. A. Litvinskii and C. Altman-Bromberg (eds.), *The Archaeology and Art of Central Asia: Studies from the Former Soviet Union*, 155-160. (Bulletin of the Asia Institute NS 8.) Bloomfield, MI:

Sagdullaev, T. and Z. A. Khakimov (1976) "Археологическое изучение городища Кызыл-Тепе (по итогам работ 1973-1974 гг.)," in V. M. Masson (eds.), *Бактрийские Древности. Предварительные сообщения об археологических работах на юге Узбекистана*, 24-30. Leningrad: Nauka. ['Archaeological Study of the Site of Kyzul-tepe (based on the work of 1973-1974),' *Bactrian*

Antiquities. Preliminary Reports on Archaeological Work in Southern Uzbekistan / Baktriiskie Drevnosti. Predvaritel'nye soobshcheniya ob arkheologicheskikh rabotakh na yuge Uzbekistana.]

Salomon, R. (1986) "The inscription of Senavarma, King of Oḍi," *Indo-Iranian Journal* 29, 261-293.

Salomon, R. (1998) *Indian Epigraphy: A Guide to the Study of Inscriptions in Sanskrit, Prakrit, and the Other Indo-Aryan Languages*. (South Asia Research.) New York; Oxford: Oxford University Press.

Salomon, R. (1999) *Ancient Buddhist Scrolls from Gandhāra: The British Library Kharoṣṭhī Fragments*. London: The British Library.

Salomon, R. (2005) "The Indo-Greek era of 186/5 BC in a Buddhist reliquary inscription," in Osmund Bopearachchi and Marie-Françoise Boussac (eds.), *Afghanistan: Ancien carrefour entre l'est et l'ouest*, 359-401. (Indicopleustoi: Archaeologies of the Indian Ocean 3.) Turnhout: Brepols.

Salvatori, S. (2008) "The Margiana Settlement Pattern from the Middle Bronze Age to the Parthian-Sasanian Period: A Contribution to the Study of Complexity," in Sandro Salvatori and Maurizio Tosi (eds.), *The Archaeological Map of the Murghab Delta II: The Bronze Age and Early Iron Age in the Margiana Lowlands: Facts and Methodological Proposal for a Redefinition of the Research Strategies*, 57-74. (BAR International Series 1806; The Archaeological Map of the Murghab Delta Studies and Reports 2.) Oxford: BAR Publishing.

Sarianidi, V. I. (1984) "Раскопки монументальных зданий на Дашлы-3," in I. T. Kruglikova (eds.), *Древняя Бактия 3: Материалы советско-афганской археологической экспедиции*, 5-32. Moscow: Nauka. ['Excavations of monumental buildings at Dashly-3,' *Drevnyaya Baktriya 3: Material'y sovetsko-afganskoi arkheologicheskie ekspeditsii.*]

Sarianidi, V. I. (1985) *Bactrian Gold: From the Excavations of the Tillya-Tepe Necropolis in Northern Afghanistan*. Leningrad: Aurora Art Publishers.

Savchuk, S. A. (1989) "Цитадель Кампыртепе," in G. A. Pugachenkova (eds.), *Античные и раннесредневековые древности Южного Узбекистана. В свете новых открытий Узбекистанской искусствоведческой экспедиции*, 73-80. Tashkent: Fan. ['The Citadel of Kampyr-tepe,' *Ancient and Early Mediaeval Antiquities of Southern Uzbekistan. In the Light of New Discoveries of the Uzbek Art-Historical Expedition / Antichnye i rannesrednevekovye drevnosti Yuzhnogo Uzbekistana. V svete novykh otkrtytii Uzbekistanskoi iskusstvovedcheskoi ekspeditsii.*]

Savoie, D. (2007) "Le cadran solaire grec d'Aï Khanoum : la question de l'exactitude des cadrans antiques," *Comptes-rendus de l'Académie des inscriptions et belles-lettres* 1161-1190.

Scerrato, U. (1980) "Due tombe ad incinerazione del Museo di Kandahar," *Annali dell'Istituto Orientale di Napoli* 40, 627–650.

Schlumberger, D. (1946) "Rapport sur une mission en Afghanistan," *Comptes-rendus de l'Académie des inscriptions et belles-lettres* 169-177.

Schlumberger, D. (1947) "Nouvelles de la délégation archéologique française en Afghanistan, fragment de poterie avec inscription grecque," *Comptes-rendus de l'Académie des inscriptions et belles-lettres* 91, 241-242.

Schlumberger, D. (1949) "La prospection archéologique de Bactres (printemps 1947) Rapport sommaire," *Syria* 26, 173-190.

Schlumberger, D. (1960) "Descendants non-méditerranéens de l'art grec," *Syria* 37, 131-166.

Schlumberger, D. (1961) *Excavations at Surkh Kotal and the Problem of Hellenism in Bactria and India*. London: Oxford University Press.

Schlumberger, D. (1965) "Aï Khanoum, une ville hellénistique en Afghanistan," *Comptes-rendus de l'Académie des inscriptions et belles-lettres* 36-46.

Schlumberger, D. (1972) "De la pensée grecque à la pensée bouddhique," *Comptes-rendus de l'Académie des inscriptions et belles-lettres* 188-199.

Schlumberger, D. and E. Benveniste (1968) "A New Greek Inscription of Asoka at Kandahar," *Epigraphia Indica* 37, 193-200.

Schlumberger, D. and P. Bernard (1965) "Ai Khanoum," *Bulletin de Correspondance Hellénique* 89, 590-657.

Schlumberger, D., M. Le Berre and G. Fussman (1983) *Surkh Kotal en Bactriane*. (Mémoires de la Délégation archéologique française en Afghanistan 25.) Paris: Diffusion de Boccard.

Schmitt, R. (1990) "Ex Occidente Lux: Griechen und griechische Sprache im hellenistischen Fernen Osten," in P. Steinmetz (eds.), *Beiträge zur*

Schober, L. (1981) *Untersuchungen zur Geschichte Babyloniens und der Oberen Satrapien von 323 – 303 v. Chr.* Frankfurt am Main: P. D. Lang.

Sedov, A. V. (1987) *Кобадиан на пороге раннего средневековья*. Moscow: Nauka.

Seldeslachts, E. (2004) "The End of the Road for the Indo-Greeks?," *Iranica Antiqua* 39, 249-296.

Senior, R. C. and D. MacDonald (1998) *The Decline of the Indo-Greeks: A Re-Appraisal of the Chronology From the Time of Menander to that of Azes.* (Monographs of the Hellenic Numismatic Society 2.) Athens:

Shaked, S. (1969) "Notes on the new Aśoka inscription from Kandahar," *Journal of the Royal Asiatic Society* 118-122.

Shaked, S. (2003) "De Khulmi à Nikhšapaya : les données des nouveaux documents araméens de Bactres sur la toponymie de la région (IVe siècle av. n. è.)," *Comptes-rendus de l'Académie des inscriptions et belles-lettres* 1517-1535.

Shaked, S. (2004) *Le satrape de Bactriane et son gouverneur: Documents araméens du IVe s. avant notre ére provenant de Bactriane.* (Persika 4.) Paris: de Boccard.

Sharif, M. (1969) *Excavation at Bhir Mound, Taxila.* (Pakistan Archaeology 6.) Karachi: Department of Archaeology.

Sharma, G. R. (1980) *Reh Inscription of Menander and the Indo-Greek Invasion of the Gaṅgā Valley.* (Studies in History, Culture and Archaeology 1.) Allahabad: Abinash Prakashan.

Shenkar, M. (2007) "Temple Architecture in the Iranian World before the Macedonian Conquest," *Iran and the Caucasus* 11, 169-194.

Sherkova, T. A. (1981) "Скульптура Египетского Божества из Могильника Туп-Хона (Южный Таджикистан," *Вестник Древней Истории* 1981/1, 73-80. ['Statuette of and Egyptian God from Tup-Khona in Southern Tadjikistan,' *Vestnik Drevnei Istorii*.]

Sherwin-White, S. and A. Kuhrt (1993) *From Samarkhand to Sardis: A new approach to the Seleucid empire.* London: Duckworth.

Shihab, S. (June 27 2002) "Bactres, la cité d'Alexandre le grand, redécouverte en Afghanistan," *Le Monde*, 23.

Shishkina, G. V. (1972) "Эллинистическая керамика Афрасиаба," *Советская Археология* 1975, 60-79. ['The Hellenistic Ceramics of Afrasiab,' *Sovetskaya Arkheologiya*.]

Shishkina, G. V. (1994) "Ancient Samarcand: Capital of Soghd," in B. A. Litvinskii and C. Altman-Bromberg (eds.), *The Archaeology and Art of Central Asia: Studies from the Former Soviet Union*, 81-99. (Bulletin of the Asia Institute NS 8.) Bloomfield, MI:

Silvi Antonini, C. (1995) "The Dalverzin temple," in A. Invernizzi (eds.), *In the Land of the Gryphons: Papers on Central Asian Archaeology in Antiquity*, 259-268. (Monografie di Mesopotamia 5.) Firenze: Casa Editrice Le Lettere.

Sims-Williams, N. (2000) *Bactrian Documents from Northern Afghanistan. Part 1: Legal and Economic Documents.* (Studies in the Khalili Collection 3; Corpus inscriptionum Iranicarum Part 2: Inscriptions of the Selucid and Parthian periods and of Eastern Iran and Central Asia, Volume VI: Bactrian) Oxford: Nour Foundation in association with Azimuth Editions and Oxford University Press.

Sims-Williams, N. (2007) *Bactrian Documents from Northern Afghanistan. Part 2: Letters and Buddhist Texts.* (Studies in the Khalili Collection 3 (2).) London: Nour Foundation in association with Azimuth Editions.

Sims-Williams, N. (2010) *Bactrian Personal Names.* (Iranisches Personennamenbuch 2: Mitteliranische Personennamen fasc. 7.) Wien: Verlag der Österreichischen Akademie der Wissenschaften.

Sims-Williams, N. and J. Cribb (1996) "A New Bactrian Inscription of Kanishka the Great," *Silk Road Art and Archaeology* 4, 75-142.

Smith, S. T. (2003) *Wretched Kush: Ethnic Identities and Boundaries in Egypt's Nubian Empire.* London: Routledge.

Srinivasan, D. M. (2010) "Śrī-Lakṣmī in Early Art: Incorporating the North-western Evidence," *South Asian Studies* 26, 77-95.

Stančo, L. (2009) "The activities in Uzbekistan in the 2008 season: testing the Google Earth programme as a tool for archaeological prospecting," *Studia Hercynia* 13, 115-122.

Stančo, L. and e. al. (2005) "Jandavlattepa 2005. Preliminary excavation report," *Studia Hercynia* 10, 167-172.

Staviskii, B. Y. (1977) *Кушанская Бактрия: Проблемы истории и културы*. Moscow: Nauka. [*Kushan Bactria: Problems of History and Culture.*]

Staviskij, B. J. (1986) *La Bactriane sous les Kushans: Problèmes d'histoire et de culture*. Paris: Maisonneuve.

Stein, S. M. A. (1929) *On Alexander's Track to the Indus*. London: Macmillan.

Stride, S. (2001) "Le programme de prospection de la MAFOuz B dans la région du Sourkhan Darya," in P. Leriche et al. (eds.), *La Bactriane au carrefour des routes et des civilisations de l'Asie centrale: Termez et les villes de Bactriane-Tokharestan: Actes du colloque de Termez 1997*, 173-183. (La Bibliothèque d'Asie centrale 1.) Paris: Maisonneuve & Larose; IFEAC.

Stride, S. (2004) "An Archaeological GIS of the Surkhan Darya Province (Southern Uzbekistan)," *The Silk Road Newsletter* 2, Retrieved September 24 2010 from <http://www.silk-road.com/newsletter/vol2012num2012/Surkhan.htm>.

Stride, S. (2007) "Regions and Territories in Southern Central Asia: What the Surkhan Darya Province Tells Us about Bactria," in Joe Cribb and Georgina Herrmann (eds.), *After Alexander: Central Asia Before Islam*, 99-117. (Proceedings of the British Academy 133.) Oxford: Oxford University Press for the British Academy.

Stride, S., B. Rondelli and S. Mantellini (2009) "Canals versus Horses: Political Power in the Oasis of Samarkand," *World Archaeology* 41, 73-87.

Taddei, M., D. W. MacDowall and P. Callieri (2004) *Bīr-koṭ-ghwaṇḍai Interim Reports II. Imported artefacts from Bīr-koṭ-ghwaṇḍai, by Maurizio Taddei; A Cataogue of Coins from the Excavations Bīr-koṭ-ghwaṇḍai 1984-1992, by David W. MacDowall and Pierfrancesco Callieri*. (Istituto italiano per l'Africa e l'Oriente, Centro scavi e ricerche archeologiche; Alma mater studiorum - Università di Bologna, Dipartimento di storie e metodi per la conservazione dei beni culturali, Reports and Memoirs 3.) Rome: IsIAO.

Tanabe, K., A. Hori, K. Ishida, M. Tsumura, K. Yamauchi and R. Takeuchi (1996) "Excavation at Dalverzin Tepe, 1996 [in Japanese with English summary]," *Bulletin of the Ancient Orient Museum* 17, 101-122.

Tarn, W. W. (1951) *The Greeks in Bactria and India*. Cambridge: Cambridge University Press.

Tarzi, Z. (1996) "Jules Barthoux : le découvreur oublié d'Aï Khanoum," *Comptes-rendus de l'Académie des inscriptions et belles-lettres* 140, 595-611.

Tissot, F. (2002) *Kaboul, le passé confisqué : le Musée de Kaboul, 1931-1965*. Paris; Suilly-la-Tour: Paris-musées; Findakly.

Tissot, F. eds. (2006) *Catalogue of the National Museum of Afghanistan, 1931-1985*. (Arts, Museums and Monuments Series.) Paris: UNESCO Publishing.

Tolstov, S. P. and B. I. Vainberg eds. (1967) *Кой-Крылган-Кала. Памятник культуры древнего Хорезма IV в. до н. э. - IV в. ч. э.* (Труды Хорезмской археолого-этнографической экспедиции 5.) Moscow: Nauka. [*Koi-Krylgan-Kala. A Monument of the Culture of Ancient Khorezm, 4th Century BC - 4th Century AD*]

Tourgounov, B. (2001) "Nouvelles données sur le site de Dalverzine-Tepe," in P. Leriche, C. Pidaev, M. Gelin, K. Abdoullaev and V. Fourniau (eds.), *La Bactriane au carrefour des routes et des civilisations de l'Asie centrale: Termez et les villes de Bactriane-Tokharestan: Actes du colloque de Termez 1997*, 241-244. (La Bibliothèque d'Asie centrale 1.) Paris: Maisonneuve & Larose; IFEAC.

Tourgounov, B. A. (1986) "Les fortifications de Dal'verzine Tépe," in Pierre Leriche and Henri Tréziny (eds.), *La fortification dans l'histoire du monde grec : actes du Colloque international La Fortification et sa place dans l'histoire politique, culturelle et sociale du monde grec, Valbonne, décembre 1982*, 283-288. (Colloques internationaux du Centre national de la recherche scientifique 614) Paris: Éditions du Centre national de la Recherche scientifique.

Trichet, J. and P. Ruben (1985) "Application de la pédologie et la géochimie à la reconstitution de l'environnement agricole de la plaine d'Aï-Khanum," in M. S. et al. Asimov (eds.), *L'archéologie de la Bactriane ancienne. Actes du Colloque franco-soviétique, Dushanbe (U.R.S.S.), 27 octobre – 3 novembre 1982*, 169-173. Paris: CNRS.

Turgunov, B. A. (1992) "Excavations of a Buddhist Temple at Dal'verzin-tepe," *East and West* 42, 131-152.

Usmanova, Z. I. (1992) "New Material on Ancient Merv," *Iran* 30, 55-63.

Ustinova, J. B. (1990) "Наскальные латинские и греческая надписи из Кара-Камара," *Вестник Древней Истории* 145-147. ['Latin and Greek Rock Inscriptions from Kara-Kamar,' *Vestnik Drevnei Istorii*.]

Vainberg, B. I. and I. T. Kruglikova (1976) "Монетные находки из раскопок Дильберджина," in I. T. Kruglikova (eds.), *Древняя Бактия: Материалы Советско-Афганской экспедиции 1969-1973 гг*, 172-182. Moscow: Nauka. ['Coins found in the Excavations of Dil'berdzhin,' *Drevnyaya Baktriya: Materialy Sovetsko-Afganskoi Ekspeditsii*.]

Vasunia, P. (2010) "Alexander Sikandar," in Susan A. Stephens and Phiroze Vasunia (eds.), *Classics and National Cultures*, 302-324. Oxford: Oxford University Press.

Vendruscolo, F. (1997) "Note testuali al papiro di Ai-Khanum," in (eds.), *Papiri filosofici: Miscellanea di studi I*, 145-151. (Studi (Accademia toscana di scienze e lettere La Colombaria) 163; Studi e testi per il Corpus dei papiri filosofici greci e latini 8.) Firenze: L. S. Olschki.

Veuve, S. (1982) "Cadrans solaires gréco-bactriens à Aï Khanoum (Afghanistan)," *Bulletin de Correspondance Hellénique* 106, 23-51.

Veuve, S. (1987) *Fouilles d'Aï Khanoum VI. Le gymnase. Architecture, céramique, sculpture.* (Mémoires de la Délégation Archéologique Française en Afghanistan 30.) Paris: De Boccard.

Vogelsang, W. (1985) "Early Historical Arachosia in South-East Afghanistan: Meeting-Place Between East and West," *Iranica Antiqua* 20, 55-99.

Vogelsang, W. J. (1988) "A Period of Acculturation in Ancient Gandhara," *South Asian Studies* 4, 103-113.

Vogelsang, W. J. (1992) *The Rise and Organisation of the Achaemenid Empire: The Eastern Iranian Evidence.* (Studies in the History of the Ancient Near East 3.) Leiden; New York: E. J. Brill.

Watson, B. (1993) *Records of the Grand Historian by Sima Qian. Han Dynasty II.* (Records of Civilization 65.) Hong Kong; New York: Research Centre for Translation, the Chinese University of Hong Kong; Columbia.

Wheeler, M. (1962) *Chārsada: A Metropolis of the North-West Frontier.* Oxford: Oxford University Press.

Wheeler, M. (1968) *Flames Over Persepolis: Turning Point in History.* London: Weidenfeld and Nicolson.

White, R. (1991) *The Middle Ground: Indians, Empires, and Republics in the Great Lakes Region, 1650-1815.* (Cambridge Studies in North American Indian History.) Cambridge: Cambridge University Press.

Whitehouse, D. (1978) "Excavations at Kandahar, 1974: First Interim Report," *Afghan Studies* 1, 9-39.

Whitehouse, D. (2001) "Begram: The Glass," *Topoi Orient-Occident* 11, 437-449.

Whitlock, M. (18 April 2004) "Uzbekistan's Best Kept Secret," *BBC News*, <http://news.bbc.co.uk/1/hi/programmes/from_our_own_correspondent/3630167.stm>, accessed 9 October 2010.

Widemann, F. (1989a) "Deux intailles indo-grecques à caractère politique," in Tony Hackens and Ghislaine Moucharte (eds.), *Technology and Analysis of Ancient Gemstones: Proceedings of the European Workshop held at Ravello, European University Centre for Cultural Heritage, November 13-16, 1987*, 173-185. (PACT 23.) Rixensart: PACT Belgium.

Widemann, F. (1989b) "Un monnayage inconnu de type gréco-bactrien à légende araméenne," *Studia Iranica* 18, 193-197.

Widemann, F. (2001) "Phases et contradictions de la colonisation grecque en Asie centrale et en Inde du nord-ouest," *Indologica Taurinensia* 27, 215-262.

Widemann, F. (2009) *Les successeurs d'Alexandre en Asie centrale et leur héritage culturel. Essai. [Seconde édition, revue et corrigée].* Paris: Riveneuve.

Will, E. (1985) "Pour une "anthropologie coloniale" du monde hellénistique," in J. W. Eadie and J. Ober (eds.), *The Craft of the Ancient Historian: Essays in honor of Chester G. Starr*, 273-301. Lanham: University Press of America.

Williams, T., K. Kurbansakhatov and e. al. (2003) "The Ancient Merv Project, Turkmenistan. Preliminary Report on the Second Season (2002)," *Iran* 41, 139-170.

Williams, T., K. Kurbansakhatov, M. Ziebart, D. Gilbert, J. Hill, D. Hopkinson, F. Vardy, G. Puschnigg, P. Brun, A. Annaev, A. Upson, C. Cavanagh, K. May, G. Watkins, B. Alvery, A. Kurbanov, J. Keily, L. Cooke and G. Palumbo (2002) "The Ancient Merv Project, Turkmenistan. Preliminary Report on the First Season (2001)," *Iran* 40, 15-41.

Wojtilla, G. (2000) "Did the Indo-Greeks Occupy Pāṭaliputra?," *Acta Antiqua Academiae Scientiarum Hungaricae* 40, 495-504.

Young, R. J. C. (1995) *Colonial Desire: Hybridity in Theory, Culture and Race*. London: Routledge.

Young, R. J. C. (2001) *Postcolonialism: An Historical Introduction*. Oxford: Blackwell.

Young, R. S. (1955) "The South Wall of Balkh-Bactra," *American Journal of Archaeology* 59, 267-276.

Zavyalov, V. A. (2007) "The Fortifications of the City of Gyaur Kala, Merv," in Joe Cribb and Georgina Herrmann (eds.), *After Alexander: Central Asia Before Islam*, 313-332. (Proceedings of the British Academy 133.) Oxford: Oxford University Press for the British Academy.

Zeimal', T. I. (1971) "Древнеземледельческие поселение Болдай-Тепе," *История материальной культуры Таджикистана* 2, 80-100. ['The Ancient Agricultural Settlement of Boldai-tepe,' *Istoriya material'noi kul'tury Tadzhikistana*.]

www.ingramcontent.com/pod-product-compliance
Ingram Content Group UK Ltd.
Pitfield, Milton Keynes, MK11 3LW, UK
UKHW061213180426
11947UKWH00029B/2022